TIME ZONES

THIRD EDITION

DAVID BOHLKE
JENNIFER WILKIN

NATIONAL
GEOGRAPHIC
LEARNING

Australia · Brazil · Mexico · Singapore · United Kingdom · United States

NATIONAL GEOGRAPHIC LEARNING

National Geographic Learning,
a Cengage Company

Time Zones 4 Third Edition
David Bohlke and Jennifer Wilkin

Publisher: Andrew Robinson

Managing Editor: Derek Mackrell

Associate Development Editor: Yvonne Tan

Director of Global Marketing: Ian Martin

Senior Product Marketing Manager: Anders Bylund

Heads of Regional Marketing:
    Charlotte Ellis (Europe, Middle East and Africa)
    Kiel Hamm (Asia)
    Irina Pereyra (Latin America)

Senior Production Controller: Tan Jin Hock

Associate Media Researcher: Jeffrey Millies

Senior Designer: Lisa Trager

Operations Support: Rebecca G. Barbush,
    Hayley Chwazik-Gee

Manufacturing Planner: Mary Beth Hennebury

Composition: Symmetry Creative Productions, Inc.

Student's Book with Online Practice
ISBN: 978-0-357-42171-0

Student's Book
ISBN: 978-0-357-41987-8

National Geographic Learning
200 Pier 4 Boulevard
Boston, MA 02210
USA

Locate your local office at **international.cengage.com/region**

Visit National Geographic Learning online at **ELTNGL.com**
Visit our corporate website at **www.cengage.com**

Printed in Mexico
Print Number: 03   Print Year: 2022

CONTENTS

SCOPE AND SEQUENCE

UNIT	FUNCTIONS	GRAMMAR	VOCABULARY	PRONUNCIATION	READ, WRITE, & WATCH
1 I LOVE MIXING MUSIC!					**PAGE 6**
	Talking about hobbies and interests **Real English:** *Tell me about it!*	**Using verb + -ing:** *Do you like playing chess? I enjoy doing jigsaw puzzles. Baking is a lot of fun.*	Hobbies Interests Nouns and verbs: *effect* vs. *affect, advice* vs. *advise, council* vs. *counsel*	Question intonation	**Reading:** Turning Hobbies into Cash **Writing:** Description **Video:** Robot Games
2 HOW LONG HAVE YOU BEEN DOING ARCHERY?					**PAGE 18**
	Identifying different sports Talking about sports and exercise **Real English:** *Give it a try.*	**Present perfect progressive:** *He's been playing tennis. I've been going to the gym.* **Adverbs of time:** *lately, recently, for, since*	Sports Collocations with *record*	Review: weak form of *been*	**Reading:** Running a Marathon **Writing:** Biography **Video:** Life Rolls On
3 WHAT SHOULD I DO?					**PAGE 30**
	Asking for and giving advice Talking about possible careers **Real English:** *On top of that, …*	**Modals for giving advice:** *should, could* **Verbs with *try*:** *try talking, try asking* **Other expressions:** *Why don't you … ? If I were you, …*	Problems and advice Phrasal verbs with *make*	Weak forms of *could* and *should*	**Reading:** Vision of Hope **Writing:** Informal letter **Video:** Eco-Fuel Africa
4 THE KOALA WAS TAKEN TO A SHELTER					**PAGE 42**
	Talking about animal rescue **Real English:** *It's up to you.*	**Passive voice without an agent:** *The dog was left at the shelter. Tags are being attached to the birds. How often are the animals fed?*	Wild animals Animal rescue Transitive and intransitive verbs	Intonation in a series	**Reading:** Bear Rescue **Writing:** News article **Video:** Raising Pandas
5 HOW ARE THEY MADE?					**PAGE 54**
	Describing manufacturing processes **Real English:** *I don't get it.*	**Passive voice with an agent:** *The wood is cut by a machine. The colors were chosen by the customer. The shoes have been customized by the store.*	Manufacturing and assembly Collocations with *global*	Contrastive stress	**Reading:** Where Is the iPhone Made? **Writing:** Descriptive paragraph **Video:** Prosthetic Legs
6 LOOK AT THOSE NARWHALS!					**PAGE 66**
	Talking about the importance of conserving marine animals and their habitats **Real English:** *You're telling me …*	**Non-defining relative clauses:** *The narwhal, which is a type of whale, has a long tusk. My uncle, who visits us every summer, is a marine biologist.*	Marine animals Coral reefs Approximation expressions	Pausing in relative clauses	**Reading:** Cities in the Sea **Writing:** Formal email **Video:** Boneless Beauties

1

I LOVE MIXING *MUSIC!*

PREVIEW

A 🎧 1.1 **Listen.** Circle each person's hobby.

		Hobby	**When**
1	Sun-hee	(drawing) / gardening	*on Sunday afternoons*
	Andy	cooking / Instagramming	
2	Eric	mixing music / dancing	
	Megan	reviewing videos / making videos	

A teenager mixes music using turntables and a sound mixer.

PEOPLE AND PLACES

B 🎧 1.1 **Listen again.** When does each person do their hobby? Fill in the **When** column in **A**.

C **Talk with a partner.** What are your hobbies? Ask follow-up questions.

UNIT GOALS

• describe your hobbies and interests

• use language for talking about things people like doing

• learn about teenagers who are making money from their hobbies

7

LANGUAGE FOCUS

A 🎧 **1.2 Listen and read.** Why doesn't Ming want to play chess? Then repeat the conversation and replace the words in **bold**.

Stig: It's so hot today. Do you feel like doing a jigsaw puzzle?

Ming: Not really. **I'm not very good at** puzzles. (**I don't really like** / **I'm pretty bad at**)

Stig: Well, how about a game of **chess**? (**Monopoly** / **Scrabble**)

Ming: Sorry, but that doesn't really sound like fun.

Stig: I know! We both **enjoy** playing sports. We can go skiing! (**like** / **love**)

Ming: I love skiing! But it's the middle of summer.

Stig: Give me just a second ...

Ming: Skiing **sure takes a lot of energy**! (**is so exhausting** / **is such good exercise**)

Stig: Tell me about it! Is it time for a break yet?

B 🎧 **1.3 Look at the chart.** Then circle the correct answers below.

TALKING ABOUT HOBBIES AND INTERESTS (USING VERB + -ING)		
What are your hobbies? What do you **like doing** in your free time?	I **love reading** comic books and fantasy novels. I **enjoy doing** jigsaw puzzles.	
Do you **like playing** chess?	Yes, I love it! Yes, I like it (a lot).	🙂
	I don't mind it.	😐
	No, I don't like it (very much). No, I can't stand it.	🙁
Skiing is such good exercise!	**Gardening** is kind of boring.	

1 After *enjoy*, we use **to + base verb** / **base verb + -ing**.

2 Base verb + *-ing* at the beginning of a sentence acts as a **noun** / **verb**.

3 If you hate doing something, you say **I don't mind it** / **I can't stand it**.

C 🎧 **1.4 Complete the conversation.** Use the correct form of the verbs in the box. Then listen and check your answers.

> dance   hike   play   sing   stay   watch

Kara: Hey, Paulo. Have you signed up for any after-school activities yet?

Paulo: No, not yet. I love [1] _____ , so I might join the musical theater club.

Kara: That would be fun! You have a great voice.

Paulo: Thanks. The problem is I don't like [2] _____ very much. I find it hard to remember all the steps. Hey! Maybe you should try out too. You enjoy [3] _____ the guitar.

Kara: Me? No way! Performing in front of people makes me nervous.

Paulo: Well, there's the Classic Film Club.

Kara: I don't really like [4] _____ old movies. Plus, [5] _____ inside even longer after school doesn't sound like fun!

Paulo: So why don't you join an outdoors club? Do you like [6] _____ ?

Kara: That's a great idea! I love the outdoors.

D 🎧 **1.5 Listen to the conversation.** What does each person think of these activities? Write 😊, 😐, or 🙁.

	baking	playing tennis	singing	playing video games
Lucia				
Wes				

E **Talk with a partner.** Look at the activities below. Do you like doing them? Why or why not?

> singing   baking   drawing   playing video games   watching TV
> gardening   reading   dancing   listening to music   doing puzzles

> I like singing a lot. I've always been good at it.

> I like singing too. I also enjoy …

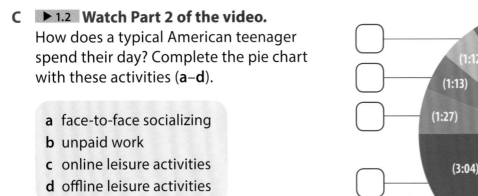

TYPICAL TEENS

A group of teens hang out and use their cell phones.

A Predict. Do you think American teenagers today spend more time (↑) or less time (↓) on these activities compared to teens 10 years ago?

_____ doing homework   _____ sleeping   _____ socializing face-to-face   _____ working for pay

B ▶ 1.1 Watch Part 1 of the video. Check your predictions in **A**. Is any of the information surprising?

C ▶ 1.2 Watch Part 2 of the video. How does a typical American teenager spend their day? Complete the pie chart with these activities (**a–d**).

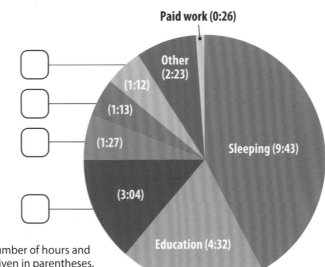

Paid work (0:26)

Other (2:23)

(1:12)

(1:13)

(1:27)

Sleeping (9:43)

(3:04)

Education (4:32)

a face-to-face socializing
b unpaid work
c online leisure activities
d offline leisure activities

Note: The number of hours and minutes is given in parentheses.

D CRITICAL THINKING Predicting **Talk with a partner.** How do you think teenagers 10 years from now will spend their time? What do you think they will do more or less of? Give reasons for your predictions.

PROJECT Create a pie chart. How do you spend a typical 24 hours? Note the number of hours and minutes you spend on each activity.

PRONUNCIATION question intonation

🎧 1.6 **Listen.** Mark each question with the intonation pattern ╱ or ╲. Then listen again and repeat the questions.

1 Do you like hiking?

2 Do you enjoy doing jigsaw puzzles?

3 Do you prefer playing board games or video games?

4 What sport do you like playing?

DO YOU KNOW?

People in _____ spend the most amount of time on leisure activities.
a the United States
b Spain
c New Zealand

COMMUNICATION

A **Look at the chart below.** Complete the sentences with information that is true for you. Then interview a classmate. Write their name and responses.

	Name: _____
I like watching _____ movies.	
I enjoy hanging out at _____.	
I don't mind spending time _____.	
I don't like playing _____.	
I enjoy listening to _____ music.	
I love _____ on weekends.	

Do you like watching horror movies?

No, I don't. I prefer watching sci-fi movies.

Where do you enjoy hanging out?

B **Work in groups.** Tell your group members the answers in your chart.

READING

A Read the title. Brainstorm possible ways people can make money from their hobbies.

B Skim the article. Of the three teenagers mentioned, who do you find most interesting? Why?

C Skim the article again. Add these headings (**a–c**) to the correct places.
   a   Helping Others Get Good Grades
   b   From Player to Developer
   c   A Tasty Road to Extra Cash

Ryan Wilson with a s'mores cake

TURNING HOBBIES INTO CASH

🎧 **1.7** They go to school, get good grades, and hang out with their friends. In most ways, they are typical teenagers. But what makes these teens different from their peers is that they have learned how to make money from their hobbies.

5 ____

Ryan Wilson, 15, learned to bake by watching online tutorials. He enjoys baking cupcakes and bread, but what he really loves creating are large, colorful cakes. He usually bakes one cake every weekend. Each cake takes about eight hours to make, and that doesn't include the time needed to
10 upload videos to his social media pages—some of which receive more than 200,000 views. After uploading the video, he shares the cake with friends and family. Ryan has **appeared** on several TV baking shows, and someday hopes to have his own show. The self-taught baker also makes money—money that will one day be used for college. And that's the real icing on the cake!

15 ____

Jasmine Shao was 13 years old when she asked her mother for permission to **post** her videos online—videos featuring calligraphy, goal planning, and study tips. At first her mother wasn't sure it was a good idea, but, after seeing how hard her daughter worked to create the videos, she **eventually** agreed.
20 Now 17, Jasmine is a social media influencer—someone who others follow, get ideas from, and even copy. Many people have viewed her videos: In 2019, she had over 270,000 Instagram followers, and 460,000 YouTube subscribers. Her success has even led to a book on study tips. "It's weird to think that I'm able to **affect** people across the country and even the world," she says.

25 ____

Luke Tesarek, 19, earned some serious cash in high school. It all started at age 13 when he first began playing video games. He quickly learned how to program games from an online tutorial and, at age 15, began to earn money as an online game programmer. He earned $8,000 that summer. Luke then
30 started work at a company as their team **leader**: The **average** age of his team was 17! At first, his mother was not happy. "I used to yell at Luke to get off the computer," she said. That began to change when she asked him how many online viewers he had. She thought he said 2,000. It was actually two million.

COMPREHENSION

IDIOM

The time that you are not working is also known as _____.
a slowtime
b backtime
c downtime

A Answer the questions about *Turning Hobbies into Cash*.

1 **REFERENCE** Who does *They* in line 1 refer to?

a all teenagers around the world

b typical American teenagers

c the teenagers mentioned in the article

2 **VOCABULARY** What's another way of saying the *icing on the cake* (line 14)?

a the extra benefit   b the main reason   c the strange result

3 **COHESION** Where is the best place for this sentence in the paragraph about Jasmine?

All this brings in extra cash.

a after sentence 1   b after sentence 2   c after sentence 3

4 **DETAIL** According to the article, whose mother used to get angry at them?

a Ryan's   b Jasmine's   c Luke's

5 **SEQUENCE** Which activity happened last?

a Luke made $8,000.

b Luke worked as a team leader.

c Luke learned how to program games.

B Look at the descriptions (a–h) below.
Write them in the Venn diagram.

a makes something you can eat
b led a team of people
c wrote a book
d watched online tutorials
e helps people plan for the future
f has been on TV
g creates their own videos
h has an online/social media presence

Ryan   Jasmine

Luke

C **CRITICAL THINKING Evaluating** **Talk with a partner.** Do you think earning money from your hobbies is a good idea? Are there downsides to what these teenagers are doing?

VOCABULARY

A **Find the bold words below in the article.** Then circle the correct answers to complete the sentences.

1 A(n) *actor / director* is someone who **appears** on TV.

2 When you **post** information on the internet, you *check it for accuracy / make it available to other people*.

3 If something **eventually** happens, it happens *immediately / after a long time*.

4 When something **affects** you, it *changes / doesn't change* you in some way.

5 The **leader** of a group of people *controls / finds problems with* it.

6 The **average** of 5, 20, and 50 is *25 / 75*.

B **Read the information below.** Then circle the correct answers.

> Some nouns and verbs in English can be easily confused with each other. For example, the verb *affect* means to have an influence on someone or something, and the noun *effect* means a consequence or result.

1 The new rule will **affect / effect** adults, but it won't have any **affect / effect** on teenagers.

2 The instructions on the box **advise / advice** users to seek medical **advise / advice**.

3 The student **counsel / council** wants teachers to **counsel / council** young people in making career decisions.

> After school, I'm usually busy with my club activities. I'm a member of the Outdoor Adventure Club. At home, I spend about four hours a day online. I like playing online games and chatting with my friends. I ...

WRITING

A **Read the paragraph.**

B **What leisure activities do you like doing?** Make a list.

C **Write a description.** Describe what you like doing in your leisure time, and how much time you spend on these activities.

ROBOT GAMES

Before You Watch

Talk with a partner. What are some things that robots can do? What would you like a robot to do for you?

While You Watch

A ▶ 1.3 **Watch the video.** Check (✓) all the things you see robots do.

- ☐ speak
- ☐ cook something
- ☐ move forward
- ☐ hang something
- ☐ carry something
- ☐ go underwater

B ▶ 1.3 **Watch again.** Circle the correct answers.

1 The FIRST Robotics Competition is for high school students from **all over the world** / **the United States**.

2 FIRST was started by Dean Kamen, a famous **athlete** / **inventor**.

3 Kamen had the idea for the competition after seeing how much kids enjoy **sports** / **robotics**.

4 A(n) **adult** / **student leader** guides each team.

C **Rank.** How well do you think robots would do in these sports? Rank them from **1** (the best) to **4** (the worst). Then share your ranking and reasons with a partner.

_____ golf   _____ skiing

_____ swimming   _____ weightlifting

After You Watch

Talk with a partner. Every year, the events at the FIRST Robotics Competition are changed to create new challenges. Make a list of challenging tasks you would like to see robots do in the competition.

Participants at the FIRST Robotics Competition

A **Match the verbs with the correct nouns to form hobbies.**

1 bake ○   ○ comic books
2 mix ○   ○ jigsaw puzzles
3 read ○   ○ music
4 do ○   ○ movies
5 watch ○   ○ cakes

B **Complete the sentences.** Use the correct form of the verbs in the box.

| cook | dance | hike | sing | spend | watch |

1 I enjoy _____ time with my friends on the weekend.

2 I can't stand _____ black-and-white movies. They're so boring.

3 I love _____. My music teacher says I have a great voice.

4 I don't mind _____, but it's not my favorite outdoor activity.

5 _____ is a lot of fun, but no one wants to eat my food!

6 I don't like _____ very much. People say I have two left feet!

C **Complete the sentences.** Use the words in the box. Two words are extra.

| advice | advise | affect | council | counsel | effect |

1 Can I give you some _____?

2 His injury had no _____ on his performance.

3 The town _____ is having a meeting right now.

4 How will the new rules _____ you?

SELF CHECK Now I can …

☐ describe my hobbies and interests

☐ talk about things people like doing

☐ talk about teenagers who are making money from their hobbies

2 HOW LONG HAVE YOU BEEN DOING ARCHERY?

PREVIEW

A 🎧 **2.1 Listen.** Match the people with the sports they do.

		Sports			How long
1 Lucy has been	○—○	playing cricket	○	○	for about two years.
2 Nathan has been	○—○	doing archery	○—○	for a year.
3 Claudia has been	○ ○	playing volleyball	○	○	since she was five.
4 Jin-soon has been	○ ○	doing taekwondo	○	○	since middle school.

An archery lesson just outside of Dublin, Ireland

B 🎧 2.1 **Listen again.** Match the people's sports in **A** with how long they have been doing them.

C **Talk with a partner.** Which sports in **A** have you done before? Which have you never done?

UNIT GOALS

- talk about sports and exercise

- use language to describe actions that continue to the present

- learn about how athletes push themselves to achieve success

19

LANGUAGE FOCUS

A 🎧 2.2 **Listen and read.** What three pieces of equipment does Stig show Nadine? Then repeat the conversation and replace the words in **bold**.

> **REAL ENGLISH** Give it a try.

Nadine: Thanks for showing me around the gym.

Stig: No problem. I've been coming here **for months**, so I know all the equipment. (**since October** / **for a long time**)

Nadine: What's this?

Stig: It's a rowing machine. It's great for working out your whole body.

Nadine: You've been using it for 10 minutes. Can I **give it a try**? (**have a turn** / **try it**)

Stig: Oh, and this bench press is good for your **upper body**. (**arms** / **shoulders**)

Stig: And here's my favorite—a chest press.

Nadine: Um, Stig, I think you're **sitting on it backward**. (**facing the wrong way** / **using it incorrectly**)

B 🎧 2.3 **Look at the chart.** Then circle the correct answers below.

DESCRIBING ACTIONS THAT CONTINUE TO THE PRESENT (USING PRESENT PERFECT PROGRESSIVE)		
Sandra looks tired. She**'s been working** hard lately.		
Nick and Tina are in great shape. They**'ve been going** to the gym a lot recently.		
How long **have** you **been doing** archery?	I**'ve been doing** it	**for** a year.
		since last year.
What **have** you **been doing** all day?	I**'ve been watching** TV.	

1   With the present perfect progressive tense, the action is **completed** / **not completed**.

2   We use **for** / **since** to indicate when an action started.

3   We use **for** / **since** to indicate how long an action has been taking place.

C Rewrite these sentences.

1 John began doing karate when he was five years old. He's still doing it now.

John _____*has been doing karate since*_____ he was five years old.

2 The snow started last night. It's still snowing now.

It _____ last night.

3 May and Etsuko started playing tennis two hours ago. They're still playing now.

May and Etsuko _____ two hours.

4 The kids began doing their homework three hours ago. They're still doing it now.

The kids _____ three hours.

5 Jessica started kayaking at 3 o'clock. She hasn't stopped yet.

Jessica _____ .

D 🎧 2.4 Complete the conversations. Circle the correct words. Then listen and check your answers.

1 **Penny:** You're really good at tennis, Carlos. Can you give me some lessons?

Carlos: Sure, but ¹ **I'm only** / **I've only been** playing ² **for** / **since** a year. How long ³ **are you** / **have you been** playing?

Penny: ⁴ **I've been** / **I was** taking lessons ⁵ **for** / **since** last month.

Carlos: Well, ⁶ **I'm** / **I've been** going to be here tomorrow at 2 o'clock. Why don't you stop by then?

Penny: Great, thanks!

2 **Ying:** You look busy, Brian. What ⁷ **are** / **were** you doing?

Brian: I'm uploading some photos to my blog.

Ying: Oh, ⁸ **are you** / **have you been** blogging long?

Brian: Not really. ⁹ **I only did** / **I've only been doing** it ¹⁰ **for** / **since** a month or so.

Ying: ¹¹ **I had** / **I've been having** a sports blog in high school. I should start it up again sometime.

E Talk with a partner. Find out about the sports your partner does. Then share the information with another classmate.

> Janet likes rock climbing. She's been rock climbing for three years. She goes to an indoor climbing gym every weekend.

THE REAL WORLD

FOOTGOLF

A footgolf player

A **Predict.** Footgolf is a new sport that is part golf and part soccer. Which of these statements about the sport do you think are true? Check (✓).

☐ It is played with a regular soccer ball.

☐ Players can use a golf club to hit the ball.

☐ It must be played on specially designed footgolf courses.

☐ Players try to get the ball into a hole.

☐ People first started playing it in Asia.

B  **▶ 2.1** **Watch the video.** Check your predictions in **A**. Correct the false statements.

C **▶ 2.1** **Watch again.** Circle the correct answers.

Similar to golf, footgolf players take the first shot from a starting area known as the [1] **tee box / fairway**. The person who is [2] **nearest to / farthest from** the hole kicks next. The players then continue until each of them kicks their ball into the hole. Players can choose to play a total of either [3] **9 or 18 / 10 or 20** holes. The player who completes the course with the fewest kicks wins.

D **CRITICAL THINKING** **Synthesizing** **Work with a partner.** Combine two sports to create a new sport. Decide on a set of rules. Then explain the rules of your sport to another pair.

PROJECT Go online. Find another "new" sport. How did the sport come about? How is it played? Share your findings with a partner.

PRONUNCIATION review: weak form of *been*

🎧 2.5 **Listen.** Write the words you hear. Then listen again and repeat the sentences.

1 He's _____ tennis since 5 o'clock.

2 She hasn't _____ to the gym much lately.

3 We've _____ here for 30 minutes.

4 People have _____ yoga for thousands of years.

COMMUNICATION

A Look at the chart. Complete the sentences. Make some of the sentences true and some false.

	True	False
I've been _____ since I was little.		
I've been _____ for a few years.		
I've been _____ a lot online recently.		
I haven't been _____ very much lately.		

B Share your sentences above with at least five people. Ask each other follow-up questions. Then mark if each person thinks the statements about you are true or false. How many people guessed correctly?

I've been playing basketball since I was little.

Really? How old were you when you started?

READING

A **Talk with a partner.** What are some things that can affect a runner's time? Why do you think runners today are faster than ever?

B **Skim paragraph C.** Are any of your ideas from **A** mentioned?

C **Scan the article.** What is the official marathon world record time as of 2019?

RUNNING A MARATHON

Eliud Kipchoge crosses the finish line to win the 2018 Berlin Marathon.

A 🎧 2.6 It's 490 B.C. The Greek army has just **defeated** a much larger Persian army at the town of Marathon, Greece. A Greek soldier named Pheidippides runs to Athens, about 40 kilometers away, to **announce** the victory. After he delivers the message, he collapses and dies. To honor his run, the marathon race was included in the first modern Olympic Games, in 1896. Since then, humans have been asking themselves how fast we can run this **distance**.

B At one point, it was believed that a runner could never run a mile (1.6 kilometers) in under four minutes. But it happened, way back in 1954. In the nearly 70 years since, the mile record has been lowered by nearly 17 seconds. In 1999, Morocco's Hicham El Guerrouj set the world record for running a mile in 3 minutes 43 seconds. As of 2019, his record still stands. Similarly, the record for running a marathon has continued to fall over the past few decades, as runners today are faster than ever.

C Researchers know what allows top runners to perform at their best. These things include a healthy diet, muscle building, pacing, and training in an ideal environment. More recently, researchers have been working to improve runners' clothing and shoes. For example, there are new socks that provide better air flow and greater foot support. Special pads on the bottom of lighter shoes help push runners forward. A new type of tape that attaches to the sides of a runner's arms and legs helps cut through the air. There is even talk of designing clothing with built-in cooling systems.

D While these things certainly help, a runner's **success** may depend on something much more difficult to measure: their level of **determination**. Kenya's Eliud Kipchoge knows this to be true. As of 2019, he is the marathon world record holder, with an official time of 2 hours, 1 minute, and 39 seconds. He set this record in 2018, breaking the **previous** record by 1 minute 18 seconds. In October 2019, Kipchoge ran the marathon distance in just under two hours; however, this did not count as an official record as the race was not an open competition. Nevertheless, Kipchoge believes it is only a matter of time before someone officially breaks the two-hour marathon barrier.

COMPREHENSION

A Answer the questions about *Running a Marathon.*

IDIOM

Something that happens "in the long run" happens _____.
a while you are running
b over a period of time
c when no one bothers you

1 **DETAIL** Which statement about Pheidippides is true?

   a He was a soldier who fought against the Greeks.

   b He ran about 40 kilometers from the town of Marathon.

   c He competed in the first modern Olympic Games.

2 **PURPOSE** What is the purpose of paragraph B?

   a to compare running a marathon with running a four-minute mile

   b to explain why it was so difficult to break the four-minute mile time

   c to talk about Hicham El Guerrouj's running achievements

3 **INFERENCE** Clothing with built-in cooling systems would be useful for runners who _____.

   a get injured easily   b usually run alone   c train in hot weather

4 **COHESION** Where is the best place for this sentence in paragraph D?

   This was the greatest improvement in a marathon record time since 1967.

   a after sentence 1   b after sentence 2   c after sentence 4

5 **INFERENCE** According to the article, which of the following is true?

   a The most important factor for success in a marathon is the use of high-tech clothing.

   b Researchers are looking into ways to measure a runner's level of determination.

   c For a marathon record to be official, the race must be open to other competitors.

B Complete the timeline below with these events (a–e).

   a The soldier Pheidippides delivered an important message.

   b Someone completed a marathon in a little over two hours.

   c The first modern Olympic Games were held.

   d Someone first ran a mile in under four minutes.

   e Someone ran an unofficial marathon in just under two hours.

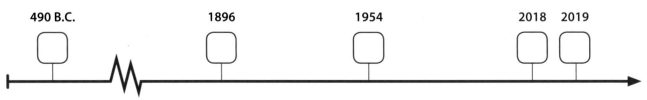

490 B.C.   1896   1954   2018 2019

C **CRITICAL THINKING Evaluating** Talk with a partner. Do you think it's fair for runners to use clothing and shoes that can enhance their performance? Why or why not?

VOCABULARY

A **Find the words below in the article.** Then complete the paragraph using the words in the box.

| announced | defeated | determination | distance | previous | success |

Hicham El Guerrouj of Morocco is one of the greatest runners of all time. He is best known for his
[1] _____ in the mile and 1,500-meter events. In 1999, he broke the world record for
the mile, running the [2] _____ in just 3 minutes 43 seconds. Despite being considered
one of the favorites to win the 1,500-meter race in the 1996 and 2000 Olympic Games,
El Guerrouj lost both times. However, he refused to give up. His hard work and [3] _____
eventually paid off. At the 2004 Athens Olympics, El Guerrouj [4] _____ runners
much younger than himself, earning gold medals in the 1,500-meter and 5,000-meter events.
His double win felt particularly satisfying after his [5] _____ losses. Shortly after,
El Guerrouj [6] _____ his retirement.

B **Read the information below.** Then circle the correct answers.

> There are many expressions containing the word *record*:
>
> | *hold the record* | *set the record* | *world record* | *medical record* |
> | *break the record* | *in record time* | *permanent record* | *financial record* |

1 As of 2019, the **permanent** / **world** record for running 100 meters is 9.58 seconds.

2 He managed to finish his homework in **record time** / **the medical records**.

3 How long did she **break** / **hold** the record for the fastest time?

WRITING

A **Read the paragraph.**

B **Choose an athlete who broke a world record.** Make notes about their achievement. Add any other biographical details (e.g., date and place of birth).

C **Write a biography.** Use your notes from **B** to help you.

Danny Way was born in 1974. He has been skateboarding for most of his life. He holds the world record for the highest jump from a ramp. Way reached a height of ...

LIFE *ROLLS* ON

Before You Watch

Take a quiz. What do you know about spinal cord injury (SCI)? Circle **T** for true or **F** for false.

1	Traffic accidents are a leading cause of SCI.	T	F
2	Over 17,000 new SCI cases occur each year in the United States.	T	F
3	Most SCI patients are female.	T	F

While You Watch

A ▶ 2.2 **Watch the video.** How does Life Rolls On help people with disabilities experience the joy of skating? Check (✓) the ways mentioned.

☐ by providing special adaptive equipment

☐ by building specially designed skate parks

☐ by training volunteers to help disabled skaters

☐ by getting professional wheelchair skaters to offer guidance

B ▶ 2.2 **Watch again.** Match each person with their description.

1 Jesse ○   ○ a 7-year-old participant at Life Rolls On
2 Will   ○   ○ the founder of Life Rolls On
3 David ○   ○ a professional wheelchair skater

C **Look at these expressions from the video.** Choose the correct meanings of the words in **bold**.

1 "It wants to show people that life **rolls on**."
   a continues   b has its ups and downs   c is like a circle

2 "I think we all **killed it**."
   a made a lot of noise   b did it very well   c got into an accident

3 "I'm **stoked** to be here."
   a nervous   b surprised   c very excited

After You Watch

Talk with a partner. Do you know of organizations similar to Life Rolls On? What do they do?

Participants at the "They Will Skate Again" event

A Do these sports use a ball? Write **B** (ball) or **NB** (no ball).

_____ archery   _____ basketball

_____ footgolf   _____ taekwondo

_____ tennis   _____ kayaking

_____ volleyball   _____ cricket

_____ skateboarding   _____ rock climbing

B Complete the sentences. Write the correct form of the verbs in parentheses. Then circle *for* or *since*.

1 Luiz _____ (**wait**) for you **for** / **since** half an hour.

2 Bryan _____ (**do**) yoga **for** / **since** 2015.

3 Mei-ling _____ (**take**) tennis lessons **for** / **since** a month.

4 Erika and Liam _____ (**work**) on their project **for** / **since** Monday.

C Complete the sentences. Use the phrases in the box.

break the record	in record time
financial records	set a record

1 He completed the race _____ .

2 They recently _____ in the relay race.

3 She managed to _____ by 0.5 seconds.

4 If you run your own business, it's important that you keep accurate _____ .

SELF CHECK   Now I can ...

☐ talk about sports and exercise

☐ describe actions that continue to the present

☐ discuss how athletes push themselves to achieve success

WHAT SHOULD
I DO?

A high school student speaks with a guidance counselor.

PREVIEW

A 🎧 **3.1 Listen.** Match the people with their problems.

1 Carrie ○   ○ has a friend who's being bullied.
2 Tomas ○   ○ doesn't know what career to pursue.
3 Keiko ○   ○ gets poor grades in algebra.

B 🎧 **3.2 Predict what advice the people in A will receive.** One piece of advice below is extra. Then listen and write the number for each person (**1–3**). Were your predictions correct?

_____ talk to your parents

_____ talk to your teacher

_____ talk to other classmates

_____ talk to the principal

C Talk with a partner. Do you agree with the advice in **B**? If not, what advice would you give?

> I don't think Tomas received good advice. I think he should …

> I think Keiko received good advice, but she could also …

PEOPLE AND PLACES

UNIT GOALS

- talk about possible careers

- learn language for asking for and giving advice

- learn about people who have achieved success in their careers

LANGUAGE FOCUS

A 🎧 3.3 **Listen and read.** What advice does Maya give Nadine? Then repeat the conversation and replace the words in **bold**.

> **REAL ENGLISH** On top of that, …

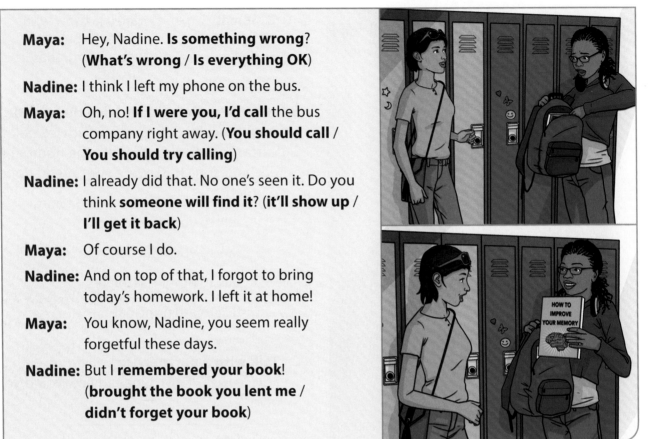

Maya: Hey, Nadine. **Is something wrong?** (**What's wrong / Is everything OK**)

Nadine: I think I left my phone on the bus.

Maya: Oh, no! **If I were you, I'd call** the bus company right away. (**You should call / You should try calling**)

Nadine: I already did that. No one's seen it. Do you think **someone will find it**? (**it'll show up / I'll get it back**)

Maya: Of course I do.

Nadine: And on top of that, I forgot to bring today's homework. I left it at home!

Maya: You know, Nadine, you seem really forgetful these days.

Nadine: But I **remembered your book**! (**brought the book you lent me / didn't forget your book**)

B 🎧 3.4 **Look at the chart.** Then circle the correct answers below.

ASKING FOR AND GIVING ADVICE (USING MODALS)	
I left my phone on the bus. **What should I do?**	You **should call** the bus company.
	You **could call** your number.
I don't know what career to pursue. **What do you suggest I do?**	You **could try talking** to a guidance counselor.
	Why don't you do some online research?
I'm not doing very well in my algebra class.	**Have you thought about getting** a tutor?
I'd like to get a new phone, but I can't afford it.	**If I were you, I'd continue** using your current phone.

1 We use the modal *should* to say that it is **necessary / a good idea** to do something.

2 After modals *could* and *should*, we use **base verb** / **to + base verb**.

3 When we say *If I were you*, the next clause uses **will** / **would** + base verb.

C **Complete the sentences.** Circle the correct answers.

1 I'm having trouble finding a good part-time job. What **could** / **should** I do?

2 Fatima wants to improve her English. Maybe she **could** / **would** take some lessons.

3 Talia's having trouble making friends at her new school. I think she **would** / **should** join a club.

4 I heard you want to adopt a cat. If I were you, I **could** / **would** call the animal shelter.

D **🎧 3.5** **Complete the conversations.** Unscramble the words. Then listen and check your answers.

1 **Joni:** Oh, no! I forgot my friend's birthday yesterday.

   Ahmed: (*her / don't / you / text / a / why / send*) ¹ _____ ?
   Wish her a belated happy birthday. I'm sure she'll understand.

2 **Chen:** I got into a big argument with my friend, and now we're not talking.

   Noreen: (*thought / about / have / apologizing / you*)
   ² _____ ?

   Chen: Not really. I don't think I should be the one apologizing.

3 **Matt:** I didn't have time to finish my math homework. (*I / do / suggest / do / what / you*)
   ³ _____ ?

   Gina: (*teacher / you / try / to / your / could / talking*)
   ⁴ _____ . He might give you an extension.

E **Write an example for each category below.** Then turn to page 150 and follow the instructions.

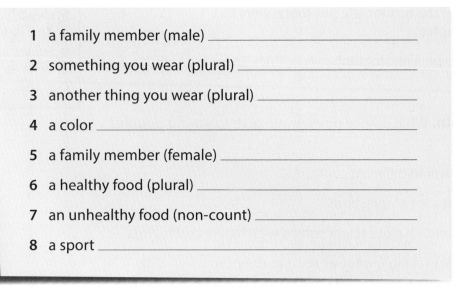

1 a family member (male) _____

2 something you wear (plural) _____

3 another thing you wear (plural) _____

4 a color _____

5 a family member (female) _____

6 a healthy food (plural) _____

7 an unhealthy food (non-count) _____

8 a sport _____

DREAM JOB

Annie Griffiths is an award-winning National Geographic photographer.

A ▶ 3.1 **Watch the video.** Circle **T** for true or **F** for false.

1 Annie takes photos of people in developing countries. **T** **F**

2 Annie was one of the first female photographers for **T** **F**
National Geographic.

3 Annie wanted to be a photographer ever since she was **T** **F**
in high school.

DO YOU KNOW?

The fastest-growing job in the United States is _____.
a app developer
b solar panel installer
c nurse

B ▶ 3.1 **Watch again.** What advice does Annie give to young people? Check (✓).

☐ They should travel to different countries.

☐ They should ask a lot of questions.

☐ They should maintain close relationships with family and friends.

☐ They should start saving money as soon as they can.

☐ They should spend more time developing their creative side.

C **Rank.** Below are some of the top dream jobs of American teenagers. How happy would you be doing these jobs? Rank them from **1** (happiest) to **6** (least happy). Then compare with a partner.

_____ music star

_____ actor/actress

_____ professional athlete

_____ jet pilot

_____ video game tester

_____ CEO of your own company

D **CRITICAL THINKING Reflecting** **Talk with a partner.** What is your dream job? What do you think would be the most challenging parts of the job?

PROJECT Talk to two adults. Ask them what they like and don't like about their jobs. Share their answers with a partner.

PRONUNCIATION weak forms of *could* and *should*

🎧 **3.6** **Listen.** Write the words you hear. Then listen again and repeat the sentences.

1 You _____ to your teacher about it.

2 I think you _____ your parents for advice.

3 I think you _____ your friend now and apologize.

4 You _____ a summer job.

COMMUNICATION

Work in groups. Choose three problems below. Take turns asking for and giving advice.

I have no idea what I want to study in college.

I'm not sure if I can afford to go to college.

I want to get a part-time job, but my parents are afraid it will affect my grades.

I've been having trouble sleeping lately.

I find it hard to balance my schoolwork and my after-school activities.

Someone I know is being bullied online.

I have no idea what I want to study in college. What should I do?

Have you tried talking to a career counselor?

READING

A **Scan the article.** By what age did Molly become completely blind?

B **Skim the article.** Underline three of Molly's accomplishments.

C **Talk with a partner.** Would you be interested in joining the organization Me to We? Why or why not?

Molly Burke speaks at We Day in Toronto, Canada.

VISION OF HOPE

🎧 **3.7** Molly Burke was not born blind. She started losing her sight when she was four years old. Doctors said that she had a rare eye disease that would **gradually** take away her vision. In first grade, she learned to read Braille, although she
5 could still see. Life was pretty normal for the next few years.

However, in seventh grade, things got worse. Black turned to gray. Yellow turned to white. Soon, Molly couldn't see the blackboard. "I just started to cry," remembers Molly. As she began to lose her vision, she started using a cane to help her
10 walk. By age 14, Molly was completely blind. Her classmates soon stopped inviting her to do things. A group of girls— girls who were once her friends—started bullying her. They even accused her of making up her blindness to get attention. Eventually, Molly became depressed. Her high
15 school years were not easy.

After she finished high school, Molly thought about what she wanted to do before college. Her brother was working in a children's home in Africa, and she wanted to do something that would help others, too. Then she found out about Me to
20 We, an **organization** that runs international volunteer trips and leadership camps. She joined the organization on a youth trip to Kenya to help build a school. While there, she spoke at a local girls' school. Molly now knew what she wanted to do next—to help inspire people by being a
25 speaker at Me to We.

Molly began speaking at schools all over the United States and Canada. Her advice? Be strong! During a speech in Toronto, she spoke to about 20,000 people. After her speech, the crowd stood up and clapped. "Molly has a real **ability** to
30 inspire people and to help others," her father says.

In 2014, Molly started her own YouTube channel, uploading things like makeup video blogs, or vlogs. As of 2019, she has close to two million subscribers, some of whom don't even know she's blind. She tries to be a **role model** for young
35 people, but is **realistic** about what she can and can't do. She even makes fun of the **challenges** she faces as a blind person—like tweeting that she once bit into a lemon, thinking it was a potato.

In 2018, Molly moved out of her parents' home and into her
40 own apartment in Los Angeles, where she still lives today. "How can you hold somebody like that back?" says her mother. "She's unstoppable."

COMPREHENSION

A Answer the questions about *Vision of Hope*.

1 **GIST** What could be another title for the article?

   a A High School YouTube Star

   b An Inspiring Role Model

   c How Molly Regained Her Vision

2 **INFERENCE** Which period of time was probably the most difficult for Molly?

   a elementary school   b high school   c college

3 **CAUSE-EFFECT** What led Molly to want to become a motivational speaker?

   a She gave a speech in Toronto.

   b She got positive feedback from her YouTube channel.

   c She spoke at a girls' school in Kenya.

4 **PURPOSE** Why does the author mention Molly mistakenly biting into a lemon?

   a to show that people sometimes still play tricks on Molly

   b to show that Molly has a sense of humor about her daily challenges

   c to show that there are still many things Molly cannot do

5 **INFERENCE** How does Molly's mother feel about her moving out?

   a She's supportive of the decision.

   b She's supportive, but feels that Molly is making a mistake.

   c She's not supportive, but knows there is no stopping Molly.

> **IDIOM**
>
> Something that provides you with a small amount of hope is called a _____ .
> a rock of hope
> b ring of hope
> c ray of hope

B Complete the timeline below with these events (a–f).

a started a YouTube channel   d learned to read Braille
b began to go blind   e became completely blind
c went on a youth trip to Kenya   f moved to Los Angeles

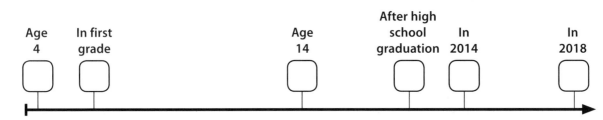

| Age 4 | In first grade | Age 14 | After high school graduation | In 2014 | In 2018 |

C **CRITICAL THINKING Reflecting** **Talk with a partner.** If you could interview Molly Burke, what questions would you ask her? Make a list.

VOCABULARY

A **Find the words below in the article.** Then complete the paragraph using the words in the box.

> ability   challenges   gradually   organization   realistic   role model

Molly Burke is a(n) ¹ _____ for people everywhere. Due to a rare disease, she lost the ² _____ to see at age 14. Her next few years of high school were difficult and full of ³ _____. She was bullied by classmates so badly that she became depressed. But with the support of her family, she ⁴ _____ recovered. After graduation, she wanted to share her story and help other victims of bullying, so she decided to become a motivational speaker for the ⁵ _____ Me to We. Since then, Molly has worked to educate others about disabilities, both physical and mental. She has even launched her own YouTube channel, where she posts regular vlogs and beauty videos. While she is careful to set ⁶ _____ goals for herself, Molly doesn't let her disability prevent her from doing the things she loves.

B **Read the information below.** Then circle the correct answers.

> Phrasal verbs are two- or three-word verbs. These phrasal verbs include the verb *make*:
>
> *make up* = to invent or imagine   *make out* = to see or hear clearly
>
> *make of* = to understand or judge   *make up for* = to make a bad situation better

1 I hear a woman's voice, but I can't make **up** / **out** what she's saying.

2 He bought her flowers to make **of** / **up for** being late.

3 I don't believe Ian's story. Do you think he made it **up for** / **up**?

4 What do you make **of** / **out** our new classmate?

WRITING

A **Read the letter.**

B **Imagine you were 13 years old again.** What would you do differently? What are some things you wish you knew back then? Note your ideas.

C **Write a letter to your 13-year-old self.** Give yourself advice.

| HOME | ABOUT US | BLOG | FAQ | CONTACT US |

Dear Walt,

I'm writing this letter to you, my 13-year-old self. I'm currently 16 years old, and I think I can offer you some good advice. Your early teens will be a difficult time, but you shouldn't be afraid to fail. You should also study hard. If I were 13 again, I'd try to …

ECO-FUEL AFRICA

Before You Watch

Take a quiz. What do you know about Uganda? Circle the correct answers.

1 The capital city of Uganda is **Kira** / **Kampala**.

2 Uganda's biggest export is **coffee** / **fuel**.

3 About **40** / **80** percent of the population lives in rural areas.

4 **English** / **French** is one of its national languages.

While You Watch

A ▶ 3.2 **Watch the video.** What could be another title for the video?

a Fuel Shortages in Uganda: Effects and Solutions

b Improving Fuel Storage Sites in Uganda

c A New Fuel for Cooking

B ▶ 3.2 **Watch again.** What are the advantages of Sanga Moses's eco-fuel? Check (✓) the ones mentioned in the video.

☐ burns cleaner   ☐ saves forests   ☐ creates bigger fires

☐ burns longer   ☐ is cheaper   ☐ can be reused many times

C **Put the events in order (1–6).**

_____ Sanga Moses quit his job.

_____ Sanga Moses spent all his savings.

_____ Sanga Moses created a clean fuel using farm waste.

_____ Sanga Moses saw his sister collecting wood.

_____ Sanga Moses became CEO of Eco-Fuel Africa.

__3__ Sanga Moses got some advice from a professor.

After You Watch

Talk with a partner. Sanga Moses's advice to teens is to "follow your heart." What does this mean? Do you think this is good advice? Why or why not?

Sanga Moses

A Complete the sentences. Circle the correct answers.

1   If you're sorry, it's a good idea to **apologize** / **get a summer job**.

2   If you aren't sure what to do, it's OK to **pursue a career** / **ask for advice**.

3   A **bully** / **role model** is someone who often hurts or frightens other people.

4   Something that is not easy to do is a(n) **challenge** / **ability**.

5   If you're realistic, you're **scared and worried** / **sensible and practical**.

B Complete the sentences. Use the words in the box.

> could   don't   should   suggest   tried   were

1   Have you _____ telling your friend how you feel?

2   It's getting late. I think you _____ call a taxi to get home.

3   I can't find my keys. What do you _____ I do?

4   There are a lot of ways to earn money. You _____ tutor someone in English.

5   If I _____ you, I'd tell the teacher the truth.

6   Why _____ you talk to someone about your problem?

C Complete the phrasal verbs in these sentences. Use up to two words for each blank.

1   What do you make _____ what the principal said this morning?

2   The story he told you wasn't real—he made it all _____.

3   Nothing can make _____ his bad behavior.

SELF CHECK   Now I can …

☐ talk about possible careers

☐ ask for and give advice

☐ talk about people who have achieved success in their careers

THE KOALA WAS **TAKEN TO A SHELTER**

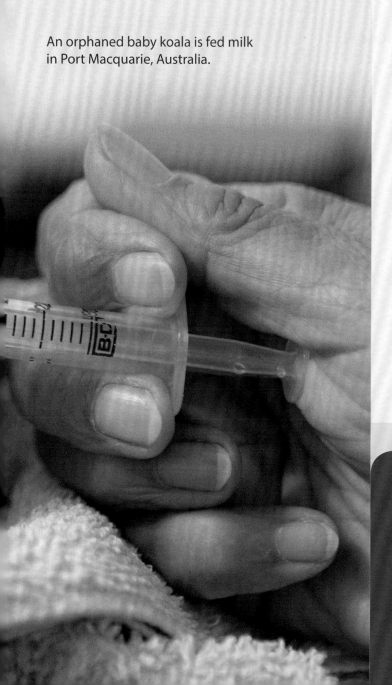

An orphaned baby koala is fed milk in Port Macquarie, Australia.

PREVIEW

A 🎧 4.1 **Listen.** What happens when an injured koala is found? Check (✓) the actions mentioned.

- ☐ It's wrapped in a blanket.
- ☐ It's placed in a cage.
- ☐ It's weighed.
- ☐ A tag is attached to it.
- ☐ It's paired with another koala.

B 🎧 4.1 **Listen again.** Circle the correct answers.

1 Wrapping the koala in a blanket helps the animal **breathe** / **calm down**.

2 It's easier to **feed** / **check for injuries on** the koala after washing it.

3 Most rescued koalas are eventually **released back into the wild** / **sent to a zoo**.

C **Talk with a partner.** Have you ever seen, or read a story about, an injured or lost animal? Explain what happened.

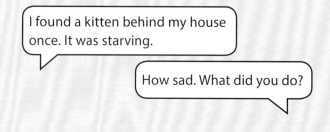

I found a kitten behind my house once. It was starving.

How sad. What did you do?

THE NATURAL WORLD

UNIT GOALS

• talk about animal rescue

• use language to describe things that are/were done

• learn about different ways to save endangered animals

43

LANGUAGE FOCUS

A 🎧4.2 **Listen and read.** What does Ming say about all the dogs at the rescue center? Then repeat the conversation and replace the words in **bold**.

> **REAL ENGLISH** It's up to you.

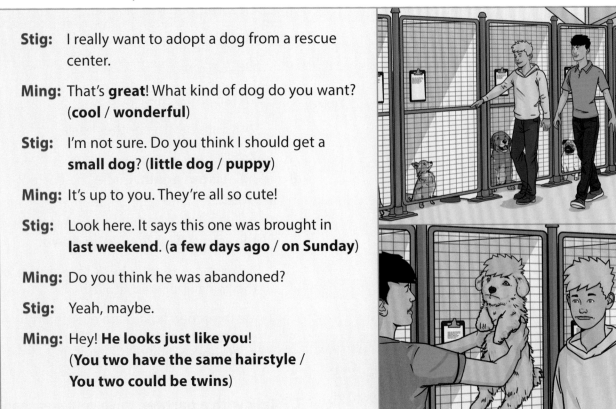

Stig: I really want to adopt a dog from a rescue center.

Ming: That's **great**! What kind of dog do you want? (**cool / wonderful**)

Stig: I'm not sure. Do you think I should get a **small dog**? (**little dog / puppy**)

Ming: It's up to you. They're all so cute!

Stig: Look here. It says this one was brought in **last weekend**. (**a few days ago / on Sunday**)

Ming: Do you think he was abandoned?

Stig: Yeah, maybe.

Ming: Hey! **He looks just like you**! (**You two have the same hairstyle / You two could be twins**)

B 🎧4.3 **Look at the chart.** Then circle the correct answers below.

TALKING ABOUT THINGS THAT ARE/WERE DONE (USING PASSIVE VOICE)	
The vet **wraps** the koala in a blanket. →	The koala **is wrapped** in a blanket.
He **is washing** the baby rabbit carefully. →	The baby rabbit **is being washed** carefully.
Someone **left** the dog at the shelter. →	The dog **was left** at the shelter.
Was the dog **abandoned**?	Yes, it was. / No, it wasn't.
How often **are** the animals **fed**?	Every four hours. / Six times a day.

1 We form the passive with the verb *be* + **present participle (e.g., *eating*)** / **past participle (e.g., *eaten*)**.

2 We use the passive to focus on the person or thing that **performs** / **experiences** an action.

3 The passive **can** / **cannot** be used when we don't know who performs an action.

C Complete the conversation. Use the correct form of the verbs in parentheses.

Max: How was your weekend, Chloe?

Chloe: Very interesting. I volunteered at the animal shelter.

Max: Really? Was it a good experience?

Chloe: It was! On Saturday, a small bird ¹ _____ (***bring***) in. Everyone thought its wings were broken.

Max: Oh, no! Did it survive?

Chloe: Yeah. It ² _____ (***give***) some medicine and then its wings ³ _____ (***check***). The vet said they weren't broken.

Max: Well, that's good. ⁴ _____ the bird _____ (***release***) after that?

Chloe: No, it's still too weak. Right now, it ⁵ _____ (***treat***) for other minor injuries. It will have to stay at the shelter until it gets stronger.

D 🎧 **4.4 Complete the information.** Use the correct form of the verbs in parentheses. Then listen and check your answers.

If you find a small, injured animal like a bird or squirrel, it probably needs medical attention. Before you ¹ _____ (***take***) the animal to a shelter, make sure it ² _____ (***cover***) with a towel or blanket. Then try to get it into a box or cage.

Line the box with some paper or old clothes to make the animal more comfortable. ³ _____ (***put***) the box somewhere dark and quiet. Once the animal ⁴ _____ (***place***) in a dark environment, it will begin to relax. Then head for the nearest shelter. Don't feed the animal.

If you find a larger animal like a deer or wild boar, you should ⁵ _____ (***call***) a rescue service for help. Never approach larger wild animals unless you ⁶ _____ (***tell***) to do so.

E Work with a partner. Student A: Turn to page 151. **Student B:** Turn to page 152.

A volunteer checks on a rescued bird.

National Geographic
Photo Ark founder
Joel Sartore with a
frill-necked lizard

ANIMAL
PORTRAITS

NATIONAL
GEOGRAPHIC

PHOTO ARK

JOEL SARTORE

A ▶ 4.1 **Watch the video.** Check (✓) the topics mentioned.

- ☐ where Joel Sartore lives
- ☐ when the National Geographic Photo Ark project was founded
- ☐ the goal of the Photo Ark project
- ☐ the number of species in the Photo Ark
- ☐ the countries Joel has traveled to

DO YOU KNOW?

Which of these animals is the most endangered?
a red kangaroo
b orangutan
c giant panda

B ▶ 4.1 **Watch again.** Circle the correct answers.

1 Joel's projects mainly deal with **wildlife conservation** / **the illegal animal trade**.

2 The animals in the Photo Ark are photographed **in the wild** / **against a plain background**.

3 In Joel's photos, small animals and big animals are presented **in the same way** / **differently**.

4 Joel feels that the Photo Ark project **is near completion** / **will continue for a long time**.

C **Rank.** On his website, Joel Sartore suggests the following ways to help save threatened animal species. Which of these are you most likely to do? Rank them from **1** (most likely) to **4** (least likely). Then compare with a partner.

_____ Donate money to a local conservation group.

_____ Support the Photo Ark by purchasing a photo or book.

_____ Volunteer with a local zoo, aquarium, or wildlife center.

_____ Share photos from the Photo Ark on your social media pages.

D **CRITICAL THINKING** **Justifying an Opinion** **Talk with a partner.** Some people think that animals shouldn't be kept in captivity. Others feel that zoos are great places to protect animals and to educate the public. What do you think? Give reasons for your opinion.

PROJECT Go to the National Geographic Photo Ark website (NatGeoPhotoArk.org) and search for an animal. Where was the photo taken? What is the animal's status? What threats does it face? Make some notes and share with a partner.

PRONUNCIATION intonation in a series

🎧 4.5 **Listen.** Mark each sentence with the intonation pattern ↗ or ↘. Then listen again and repeat the sentences.

1 The shelter was able to save a bird, a raccoon, and a rabbit.

2 The bird was picked up, wrapped in a blanket, and taken to the shelter.

3 The animal was given food, water, and medicine.

COMMUNICATION

Work in groups. Create a headline by matching information from these three columns. Include detailed information to make the story interesting. Then present your group's news story to the class.

A	B	C
An Angry Monkey Three Hungry Zebras Several Snakes Thirty Cats A Basket of Puppies A Swarm of Bees	Seen Spotted Found Discovered	at a Playground in a High School Cafeteria outside a Burning Building inside an Ice Cream Shop near the Zoo Entrance on a Cruise Ship

In today's news, several snakes were found inside an ice cream shop.

That's right. The snakes were seen …

READING

A Look at the photos. What do you think happened?

B Scan the article. Where did the bear spend the night?

C Talk with a partner. Are there wild bears in your country?
Do you know what you should do if you encounter a wild bear?

A black bear hangs on to the
arch of a bridge in California.

BEAR *RESCUE*

🎧 4.6 A black bear was in a **dangerous** situation when she fell off a 30-meter-high bridge. After a long day in California's Sierra Nevada mountains, the bear probably thought she was taking a shortcut home. She was walking across the bridge when, **suddenly**, two cars entered from both sides. There was nowhere
5 to run, so the **frightened** bear jumped onto the rail and began to fall over the side.

Luckily, the bear pulled herself onto an arch under the bridge, but she was trapped there. A driver at the scene called 911. Robert Brooks, an animal control officer from the nearby town of Truckee, was sent to **investigate**. "I thought it
10 was a joke," he said. But it wasn't a joke, so he called Dave Baker of the BEAR League—an organization that helps bears in trouble. "He thought I was playing a joke on him, too," Brooks said.

Unfortunately, the sky was getting dark, so the rescuers had to wait. Early next morning, the two men returned to the bridge with more volunteers. Amazingly,
15 the bear was still there. They needed to rescue her quickly. Baker had an idea— they should **hang** a net under the bear, push her into it, and then lower her to the ground.

Firefighters volunteered to lower the 100-kilogram bear once she was in the net. Police officers closed the road, and when the net arrived, it was hung under
20 the bridge. Then, an animal control officer shot a dart containing a sleeping drug into the bear's shoulder. Ann Bryant, head of the BEAR League, stood under the bridge. When the bear was sleepy, Bryant yelled, "OK, push!" A volunteer rock climber used his feet to push the bear off the arch, right into the middle of the net.

25 The bear was gently lowered to the ground. When she touched the ground, everyone **cheered**. Bryant and Officer Brooks guided the sleepy bear to a small river, where she could finally get a drink. "She just kind of lay down on her tummy and put her paws under her chin," said Bryant, "like a dog lying on the living room floor … only big!" The rescuers then cleared all the people from the
30 area and left the bear alone so she could sleep. Since then, no one has seen her. "I don't think she's going near that bridge anymore," Brooks said.

Rescuers use a net to carry the bear to safety.

COMPREHENSION

A Answer the questions about *Bear Rescue.*

1 **PURPOSE** The purpose of the article is to _____ .

   a teach readers about bears

   b tell an interesting story

   c persuade readers that wild bears are dangerous

2 **INFERENCE** Baker thought Brooks was joking because _____ .

   a it was an unbelievable story

   b Brooks often tells jokes

   c it was a very funny story

3 **DETAIL** Why wasn't the bear rescued immediately?

   a It got too dark.

   b The rescuers couldn't find a net.

   c There were too many cars on the bridge.

4 **INFERENCE** The rescuers had to make the bear sleep first so that she _____ .

   a could rest   **b** wouldn't feel hungry   **c** wouldn't attack people

5 **DETAIL** According to the article, who was NOT involved in the rescue?

   a a firefighter   **b** a vet   **c** a rock climber

B Put the events in order (1–7).

_____ The bear was lowered safely to the ground.

_____ Rescuers hung a net under the bridge.

_____ The bear started to fall and became stuck under the bridge.

_____ The people who were watching were all cleared from the area.

___1___ A bear was walking across a tall bridge in the Sierra Nevada mountains.

_____ The bear was shot with a sleeping dart and pushed into the net.

_____ Two cars entered the bridge, and the bear jumped onto the rail.

C **CRITICAL THINKING Evaluating** **Talk with a partner.** Can you think of other ways the bear could have been rescued?

IDIOM

If you tell someone to "hang in there," you are telling them to _____ .
a cut corners
b forget their problems
c not give up

VOCABULARY

A Find the bold words below in the article. Then circle the correct answers.

1 Something that is **dangerous** is not *safe / helpful*.

2 An event that happens **suddenly** happens *slowly and expectedly / quickly and unexpectedly*.

3 A **frightened** animal is *scared of / unsure about* something.

4 If you **investigate** a situation, you *completely ignore it / try to find out what happened*.

5 Two things you can **hang** are *a river and a tree / a towel and a painting*.

6 When people **cheer**, they are probably *happy / unhappy*.

B Read the information below. Then look at the verbs in the box. Add them to the correct column in the chart. Use a dictionary to help you.

> A transitive verb requires an object (*He <u>lowered</u> **the net**.*). An intransitive verb does not require an object (*The bear <u>fell</u>.*). Some verbs can be both transitive (*I <u>broke</u> **the plate**.*) and intransitive (*The plate <u>broke</u>.*).

arrive   bring   come   enter   help   rescue

Transitive verbs	Intransitive verbs	Transitive and intransitive verbs

WRITING

A Look at the photo. Read the beginning of the news article.

B Make notes about the photo. What does it show? What do you think happened next?

C Write a news article based on the photo. Use your notes from **B** to help you.

HOME | ABOUT US | **NEWS** | CONTACT US

A large ship began leaking oil this morning. The oil spill is threatening wildlife in the region. This bird was rescued just hours ago. Volunteers . . .

RAISING PANDAS

Before You Watch

Talk with a partner. Look at the photo. What do you know about pandas? What adjectives would you use to describe them?

While You Watch

A ▶ 4.2 **Watch the video.** Check (✓) all the things you see.

☐ A panda is wrapped in a blanket.

☐ A man lies down on the grass with pandas.

☐ People dress up as pandas.

☐ A panda is released from a cage.

B ▶ 4.2 **Watch again.** Circle **T** for true or **F** for false.

1 Zhang Hemin's center has successfully bred and released pandas.   **T**   **F**

2 Baby pandas are born blind.   **T**   **F**

3 Newborn pandas can stand on their own.   **T**   **F**

4 At the center, the survival rate for baby pandas has reached 90 percent.   **T**   **F**

C **Complete the summary below.** Use the words in the box. Two words are extra.

| alive | costumes | cubs | full | mate | predators |

It's difficult to breed pandas in captivity. First, it's hard to get them to [1] _____ . Second, they don't get pregnant easily. And third, it's not easy to keep baby pandas [2] _____ . But Zhang Hemin says that his center has solved these problems. The center also works hard to train pandas to survive on their own in the wild. One idea Zhang came up with was for staff members to wear panda [3] _____ when interacting with the animals. Pandas at the center are also trained to recognize [4] _____ .

After You Watch

Talk with a partner. Do you think tourists should be allowed to visit the panda center? Why or why not?

A Write the past participle of these verbs.

1 see _seen_

2 wrap _____

3 put _____

4 place _____

5 bring _____

6 feed _____

7 give _____

8 treat _____

9 drive _____

10 release _____

B Complete the conversation. Circle the correct answers.

Ling: Who ¹ **brought / was brought** this raccoon to the shelter?

Jack: No one ² **knows / is known**. It ³ **left / was left** at the door. My guess is that a car ⁴ **hit / was hit** it.

Ling: Oh, no! Do you think it will survive?

Jack: Yeah, I think so. ⁵ **It's being examined / It was examined** about an hour ago. I ⁶ **told / was told** it should make a full recovery.

C Read these sentences. Mark the verbs as **T** (transitive) or **I** (intransitive). If the verb is transitive, underline its object.

1 __T__ He threw <u>the ball</u> a long way.

2 _____ She arrived late this morning.

3 _____ Why don't you bring some snacks?

4 _____ You should enter the building through the side door.

5 _____ Can you come around 4 p.m. tomorrow?

6 _____ A brave neighbor rescued the dog from the fire.

Twin giant panda cubs

SELF CHECK Now I can ...

☐ talk about animal rescue

☐ describe things that are/were done

☐ discuss different ways to save endangered animals

HOW
ARE THEY MADE?

Metal tips are attached to pencils by
a machine at a factory in New Jersey.

PREVIEW

A **Read the sentences below.** Match the words in **bold** with their definitions (**a–c**).

_____ Another piece of wood is stuck on top using **glue**.

_____ An eraser is added to each pencil.

___1___ Soft wood is cut into flat pieces.

_____ **Grooves** are cut into the wood, and **lead** is put in.

_____ Each pencil is checked by hand.

_____ The pieces of wood are cut into pencils.

Definitions

a _____ : deep lines cut into a surface

b _____ : a sticky substance used to join things together

c _____ : the thin, black material in the center of a pencil

B 🎧 **5.1** **Listen.** How are pencils made? Put the steps in **A** in order (1–6).

C **Talk with a partner.** Think of another object you use every day. How do you think it is made?

> I wonder how paper is made.

> Well, paper is made from trees. So …

SCIENCE AND TECHNOLOGY

UNIT GOALS

• talk about manufacturing processes

• use language to describe how things are/were done

• learn about how technology is used in manufacturing

LANGUAGE FOCUS

A 🎧 **5.2** **Listen and read.** What is Ming thinking of getting from the store? Then repeat the conversation and replace the words in **bold**.

REAL ENGLISH I don't get it.

Ming: Check out this store, Maya. They customize sneakers.

Maya: What does that mean?

Ming: They can add a design to a pair of sneakers so they're **unique**. (**one of a kind** / **just for you**)

Maya: I don't get it. How exactly **do they do that**? (**does it work** / **is it done**)

Ming: You just buy the sneakers, and your name, design, or picture is **added** by a machine. The store can do whatever you want. (**put on** / **stitched on**)

Maya: So what are you **thinking of getting**? (**getting** / **going to get**)

Ming: I think I'll get a white pair of sneakers with a large "M" on the side. "M" for Ming.

Maya: And "M" for Maya! Maybe I'll do the same!

B 🎧 **5.3** **Look at the chart.** Then circle the correct answers below.

TALKING ABOUT HOW THINGS ARE/WERE DONE (USING PASSIVE VOICE + *BY*)	
A machine **cuts** the wood.	→ The wood **is cut by** a machine.
A factory worker **checks** the pencils.	→ The pencils **are checked by** a factory worker.
The customer **chose** the design.	→ The design **was chosen by** the customer.
A logging company **cut down** the trees.	→ The trees **were cut down by** a logging company.
The store **has customized** the shoes.	→ The shoes **have been customized by** the store.
The pencils **are made of** soft wood.	

1 We use the passive to describe what **happens to something or someone** / **something or someone does**.

2 In passive sentences, the person or thing doing the action follows **by** / **in**.

3 When describing a manufacturing process, a material such as wood or cotton usually follows **by** / **made of**.

C Rewrite these sentences.

1 A supervisor checks each item.

Each item _____ .

2 Millions of people saw the performance.

The performance _____ .

3 The teacher answered the students' questions.

The students' questions _____ .

4 Thousands of tourists have visited the national park.

The national park _____ .

5 A machine puts the cookies into boxes.

The cookies _____ .

D 🎧 5.4 Complete the paragraph. Use the correct form of the verbs in parentheses. Then listen and check your answers.

In 2018, a tiny house [1] _____ (**produce**) by ICON, a construction technology company. The house was 350 square feet and took 48 hours to build. It [2] _____ (**create**) using a 3D printer. A year later, the company [3] _____ (**make**) an even larger home in about 27 hours. When the company [4] _____ (**announce**) this, it [5] _____ (**consider**) by many people to be a major breakthrough. This means it is now possible to build houses quickly, which could help reduce the number of homeless people around the world.

E Work with a partner. Student A: Turn to page 153. **Student B:** Turn to page 154.

An ICON 3D-printed home

MAKING AN ARTIFICIAL EYE

A Look at the diagram below. Label the parts of the eye.

iris   pupil   vein   white

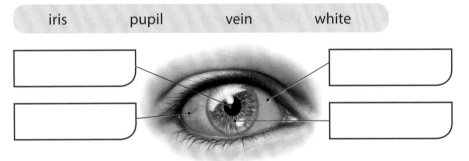

B ▶5.1 Watch the video. How are artificial eyes made? Put the steps in order (1–6).

_____ The pupil and the iris are painted.

__4__ The whole mold is heated in an oven.

_____ The white of the eye is pressed against the iris in the mold.

_____ The eye is heated again and polished.

__1__ A mold of the eye is created.

_____ The eye is trimmed, and veins are added using silk.

C Complete the information. Circle the correct answers.

An artificial eye [1] **can / cannot** restore someone's vision, but it can look very lifelike and move like a real eye. The artificial eye is attached to muscles in the eye socket so that the eye movements match those of the patient's natural eye. It is therefore often [2] **easy / difficult** to tell if a person has an artificial eye. New research using mice is giving scientists hope that they might someday [3] **develop / discover** an artificial eye that can actually see.

D [**CRITICAL THINKING** Analyzing] **Talk with a partner.** Why do you think it's necessary to add veins to an artificial eye?

> **PROJECT Look around your home.** Find five things that were made in another country. Examples may include appliances, food items, clothing, etc. Tell a partner where these things were made.

PRONUNCIATION contrastive stress

🎧 5.5 **Underline the word in each response that you think receives the most stress.** Listen and check your answers. Then repeat the questions and responses with a partner.

	Question	Response
1	Is the iris painted on by a machine?	No, it's painted by hand.
2	Can an artificial eye see?	No, an artificial eye can't see.
3	Paint is used for the veins.	Actually, silk is used for the veins.
4	Most artificial eyes are made of glass.	Well, they were made of glass, but not anymore.

COMMUNICATION

Find the people below. When you find the person, ask a follow-up question to get additional information. Write their responses in the chart.

Find someone who …	Additional information
has been chased by a dog	
has been punished by a teacher	
has been stung by a bee	
has been given flowers by a friend	
has been awarded a prize	

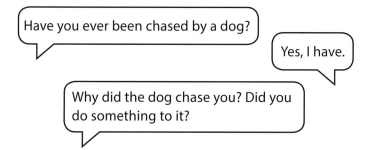

Have you ever been chased by a dog?

Yes, I have.

Why did the dog chase you? Did you do something to it?

READING

A **Skim the article and look at the map below.** Why is the question in the title difficult to answer?

B **Scan the article.** Underline all the countries mentioned.

C **Talk with a partner.** Do you own an iPhone? Why do you think iPhones are so popular?

WHERE DO IPHONE PARTS COME FROM?

SOUTH KOREA
(memory)

GERMANY
(movement
sensor)

U.S.A.
(glass screen,
audio chip,
Wi-Fi chip)

JAPAN
(camera,
compass)

CHINA
(battery)

SWITZERLAND
(positioning system)

WHERE IS THE
IPHONE MADE?

🎧 5.6 Have you ever wondered where Apple's iPhone is made? Apple's headquarters is located in California, where iPhone models are designed by a talented team of engineers and designers. So you might assume that
5 the iPhone is made by workers in the United States. However, the answer to the question is more **complex** than you may expect.

Manufacturing vs. Assembly

To answer the question, we need to understand the
10 difference between manufacturing and assembly. Manufacturing is the process of making the parts that go into the iPhone. Although Apple designs and sells the iPhone, it doesn't manufacture its **individual** parts. Instead, the company uses manufacturers from around
15 the world to **supply** these. And there are hundreds of parts—including wires, batteries, and chips. In total, Apple works with more than 200 different suppliers in over 40 countries. Among the top supplier nations are China, the United States, Japan, and South Korea.

20 Assembly is the process of taking all those individual parts and **combining** them into a finished, working iPhone. The assembly of iPhones takes place in China, which has shown itself to be good at meeting demand quickly. In 2007, for example, just a few weeks before
25 the first iPhone was released, Apple co-founder Steve Jobs decided to replace the iPhone's plastic screen with a glass screen. This new glass screen would be scratch-proof. American companies said this was impossible—they would need several months to
30 create new production lines to make the change. A Chinese factory, however, accepted the work and proved it was possible.

The Bigger Picture

"People just look at where the final product is
35 assembled," says Apple CEO, Tim Cook. According to Cook, we need to look at the bigger picture. In a **global** world, he says, manufacturing needs to be done in a **variety** of countries, so it's not easy to say exactly where a product is made. Thus, making an iPhone is
40 truly a worldwide effort.

Tim Cook, CEO of Apple, speaks at an iPhone event in California.

COMPREHENSION

IDIOM

If you "phone something in," you do an activity _____.
a with little effort or interest
b in a very complicated way
c because it's urgent

A Answer the questions about *Where Is the iPhone Made?*

1 **MAIN IDEA** What point is the author trying to make?

  a It's very difficult to manage a global supply chain.

  b Some companies don't want customers to know where their products are made.

  c It's not always easy to say where a product comes from these days.

2 **DETAIL** Where is the iPhone designed?

  a in the United States   b in China   c in Japan

3 **REFERENCE** What does *these* in line 15 refer to?

  a manufacturers   b parts of an iPhone   c finished iPhones

4 **INFERENCE** Apple probably chose to assemble iPhones in China because _____.

  a glass screens are cheaper in China

  b Chinese factories have proven to be good at meeting last-minute demands

  c more and more skilled workers are moving to China

5 **PARAPHRASE** What does Tim Cook mean when he says we need to *look at the bigger picture* (line 36)?

  a We have to create phones with larger display screens.

  b We have to keep coming up with new ideas and solutions.

  c We have to take a broad view of an issue, and not focus on small details.

B Read the statements. Circle **T** for true, **F** for false, or **NG** for not given.

1 Apple's main office is in China.   T   F   NG

2 The iPhone accounts for nearly half of Apple's sales.   T   F   NG

3 The first iPhones that went on sale had a plastic screen. T   F   NG

4 It takes about 400 steps to assemble an iPhone.   T   F   NG

5 According to the map on page 60, some parts of the   T   F   NG
   iPhone are made in Europe.

C CRITICAL THINKING Reflecting Talk with a partner. How important is your cell phone to you? At what age do you think children should have cell phones?

VOCABULARY

A **Find the bold words below in the article.** Then circle the correct answers.

1 Something **complex** is probably *easy / difficult* to understand.

2 If you look at a car's **individual** parts, you look at *each part separately / the whole car*.

3 If you **supply** a company with something, you *provide / purchase* it.

4 When you **combine** two or more things, you *mix them together / separate them*.

5 A **global** event is one that *happens only in your country / affects the whole world*.

6 If you enjoy eating a **variety** of foods, you like *many types / just one type* of food.

B **Read the information below.** Then complete the sentences (1–4) with expressions from the box.

> There are many words that are often used with *global*:
>
> global awareness   global brand   global network   global warming

1 The company has an efficient _____ in place so products can reach customers quickly.

2 The organization hopes to increase _____ of the benefits of organic products.

3 One effect of _____ is rising sea levels.

4 Apple is a well-known _____—everyone recognizes its logo immediately.

WRITING

A **Read the paragraph.**

B **Think of an item you own that was a gift.** Make notes about it. Who gave it to you? Where was it made? What is it made of? Add any other information.

C **Write about the gift.** Use your notes from **B** to help you. Say why this item means a lot to you.

A few years ago, I was given a watch by my grandfather. It was made in Germany. He bought it when he went there on vacation. It's made of metal, but the strap is leather. It's not an expensive watch, but it means a lot to me because ...

PROSTHETIC LEGS

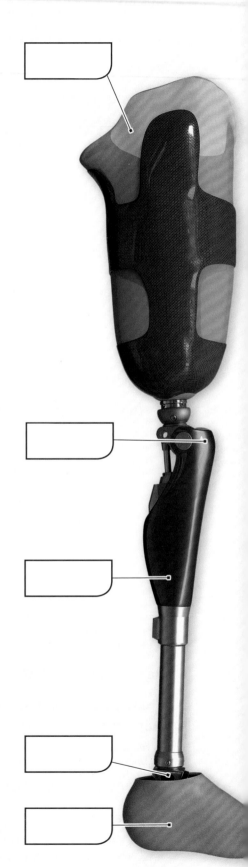

Before You Watch

Look at the diagram on the right. Label the parts of the prosthetic leg.

> ankle   foot   knee   shin   socket

While You Watch

A ▶ 5.2 **Watch the video.** Number the parts of the prosthetic leg in the order they are made (1–6).

_____ knee	_____ shin	_____ socket
__1__ foot	_____ skin	_____ ankle

B ▶ 5.2 **Watch again.** Match each body part with what it's made from.

1 foot ○   ○ aluminum

2 shin ○   ○ carbon fiber

3 ankle ○   ○ silicon

4 skin ○   ○ rubber

C **Complete the information below.** Use the words in the box. One word is extra.

> assemble   average   cost   materials   patient

All prosthetic limbs are customized according to the needs of each individual [1] _____ . A doctor takes several factors into consideration, such as the person's weight, age, and lifestyle. A new prosthetic limb can [2] _____ anywhere from $5,000 to $50,000, depending on the [3] _____ used. But even the most expensive limbs will need to be replaced after a few years. A prosthetic limb usually lasts a(n) [4] _____ of three to five years.

After You Watch

Talk with a partner. Do you think athletes with prosthetic limbs should be allowed to compete against regular athletes? Why or why not?

A Match the words with their definitions.

1 assemble   ○   ○ to produce something on a large scale

2 stitch   ○   ○ to make something unique

3 customize   ○   ○ to provide

4 manufacture   ○   ○ to put the parts of an object together

5 supply   ○   ○ to join or decorate using a needle and thread

B Complete the sentences. Use the correct form of the verbs in the box.

choose	design	leave	make

1 This building _____ by a team of three architects. They won an award for their creation.

2 This shirt _____ of Egyptian cotton. Feel how soft it is.

3 Last week, our city _____ as the host city for the conference.

4 These books _____ here a week ago. Can you please put them away?

C Complete the sentences. Circle the correct answers.

1 Coca-Cola is a global **brand** / **awareness**.

2 Scientists worldwide agree that global **warming** / **brand** is happening and that human activity is the main cause.

3 The company has built up a global **warming** / **network**, with a presence in more than 80 countries.

SELF CHECK   Now I can ...

☐ talk about manufacturing processes

☐ describe how things are/were done

☐ discuss how technology is used in manufacturing

LOOK AT THOSE
NARWHALS!

Narwhals are often called the "unicorns of the sea."

PREVIEW

A 🎧 6.1 **Listen.** Check (✓) the ocean(s) each animal lives in: Atlantic (**At**), Pacific (**P**), Indian (**I**), or Arctic (**Ar**).

	At	P	I	Ar
dugong				
king crab				
narwhal				
seahorse				

B 🎧 6.1 **Listen again.** Complete the sentences with words from the box.

> flippers   shells   tail   tusk

1 The dugong, which is a kind of mammal, uses its _____ for steering while swimming.

2 King crabs, which have red, blue, or brown _____, are caught for food.

3 The narwhal, which has a long, straight _____, is a type of whale.

4 The seahorse, which is a type of fish, uses its _____ to move forward.

C **Talk with a partner.** Make a list of all the sea creatures you know about. Which ones have you seen?

THE NATURAL WORLD

UNIT GOALS

- talk about marine animals and their habitats

- use language to add information about things and people

- learn about the importance of coral reefs

LANGUAGE FOCUS

A 🎧6.2 **Listen and read.** What kind of shells do hermit crabs usually live in? Then repeat the conversation and replace the words in **bold**.

REAL ENGLISH You're telling me …

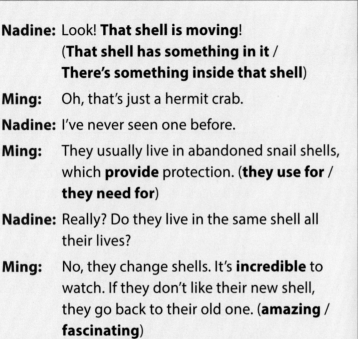

Nadine: Look! **That shell is moving!** (**That shell has something in it** / **There's something inside that shell**)

Ming: Oh, that's just a hermit crab.

Nadine: I've never seen one before.

Ming: They usually live in abandoned snail shells, which **provide** protection. (**they use for** / **they need for**)

Nadine: Really? Do they live in the same shell all their lives?

Ming: No, they change shells. It's **incredible** to watch. If they don't like their new shell, they go back to their old one. (**amazing** / **fascinating**)

Nadine: So, you're telling me they want the **most fashionable** shell-ter! (**most stylish** / **coolest-looking**)

B 🎧6.3 **Look at the chart.** Then circle the correct answers below.

ADDING INFORMATION TO A SENTENCE (USING NON-DEFINING RELATIVE CLAUSES)
The narwhal, **which is a type of whale**, has a long tusk.
The dugong, **which is a kind of mammal**, is sometimes called a sea cow.
Last weekend we went to the aquarium, **which now has a collection of seahorses**.
My uncle, **who visits us every summer**, is a marine biologist.
My cousin Lisa, **who is a scuba diving instructor**, knows a lot about coral reefs.
If you have questions, ask the tour guide, **who is an expert on ocean conservation**.

1 A clause that adds extra information about a person begins with **which** / **who**.

2 A clause that adds extra information about a thing begins with **which** / **who**.

3 We use **commas** / **semicolons** to separate a non-defining relative clause from the rest of the sentence.

C 🎧 **6.4 Complete the paragraph.** Use the phrases in the box (**a–d**). Then listen and check your answers.

> **a** which is where they find all their food
> **b** which they gather with their tentacle-like feet
>
> **c** which means they're active at night
> **d** which are related to starfish and sea urchins

Sea cucumbers, ¹ _____ , are one of the ocean's most interesting creatures. There are over 1,200 known species, and they come in a variety of colors. They are typically 10 to 30 centimeters long, although the largest species can reach 3 meters. Most sea cucumbers live on the ocean floor, ² _____ . They eat algae, tiny sea creatures, and even waste materials, ³ _____ . When threatened, some sea cucumbers shoot sticky threads out of their bottoms to trap their enemies. Sea cucumbers are nocturnal creatures, ⁴ _____ .

A sea cucumber

D **Rewrite these sentences.** Use *which* or *who*.

1 Alice is writing a research paper on narwhals. She's a marine biologist.

_____Alice, who's a marine biologist, is writing a research paper on narwhals._____

2 The *Titanic* is now an underwater shelter for marine life. It sank in 1912.

_____

3 My friend Jada is coming to visit this weekend. She's studying medicine in Toronto.

_____

4 Rio de Janeiro is an interesting place to live. It has a population of more than six million.

_____

5 My science teacher is very patient and friendly. He's from Australia.

_____

E **Play a chain game.** Work in groups of three. One student says a sentence. The other two students add more information to the sentence using *which* or *who*.

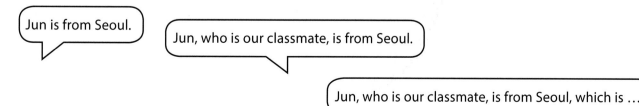

Jun is from Seoul.

Jun, who is our classmate, is from Seoul.

Jun, who is our classmate, is from Seoul, which is …

LEARNING FROM HUMPBACKS

Humpback whales have inspired new wind turbine technology (inset).

A ▶ 6.1 **Watch the video.** What characteristic of humpback whales has inspired scientists to create more efficient wind turbines?

a the blowholes on the top of a humpback's head

b the structure of a humpback's flippers

c the shape of a humpback's head

B ▶ 6.1 **Watch again.** Circle the correct answers.

1 The drag on something makes it move more **slowly** / **quickly**.

2 Wind turbines with tubercles experience **more** / **less** drag.

3 Researchers are considering adding tubercles to **the bottom of ships** / **airplane wings** to increase speed and improve safety.

DO YOU KNOW?

The nose of Japan's Shinkansen bullet trains is modeled after _____.
a a kingfisher's beak
b a narwhal's tusk
c the head of a fish

C **Read the definition of biomimicry below.** Then check (✓) the options that are examples of biomimicry.

> **biomimicry** (*n.*): the science of copying designs from nature in human engineering and invention

☐ putting bird feathers in a jacket to stay warm in cold weather

☐ inventing a multilegged robot that can move through tight spaces like a spider

☐ sticking pieces of shark skin onto swimwear to help people swim faster

☐ developing a bat-inspired drone that can fly around in the dark by itself

☐ designing a prosthetic arm that looks and functions like an octopus tentacle

D **CRITICAL THINKING Applying** **Talk with a partner.** What other traits or abilities of animals or plants do you think would be useful to copy? In what situations might these traits or abilities be useful to humans?

> **PROJECT Go online.** Find another example of biomimicry. Make some notes about it and share with a partner.

PRONUNCIATION pausing in relative clauses

🎧 6.5 **Listen.** Mark the pauses in these sentences with a slash (/). Then listen again and repeat the sentences.

1 My friend Maria/who runs the aquarium/is interested in marine conservation.

2 Saltwater crocodiles, which are very dangerous, are the largest living reptiles.

3 The scientists, who work for WhalePower, are studying humpback whales.

4 Sea otters, which live in the Pacific Ocean, are very playful animals.

COMMUNICATION

Play a guessing game. Work in groups. **Group A:** Turn to page 155. **Group B:** Turn to page 156. Follow the instructions on the page.

This animal, which can live up to 23 years, lives in the Pacific Ocean.

Is it a whale shark?

No, sorry. The next animal, which …

READING

A Read paragraph A. What are *polyps*?
  a small creatures that can cause coral reefs to become sick
  b tiny organisms that form the structure of coral reefs
  c large fish that depend on coral reefs for survival

B Skim the article. Add these headings (1–4) to the correct places.
  1 Reefs in Trouble   3 Super-Sized Cities
  2 What Can We Do?   4 Why Are Reefs Important?

C Scan the article. Underline all the things that are threatening the health of coral reefs.

The Great
Barrier Reef,
Australia

CITIES IN THE SEA

A 🎧 6.6 They may be small, but they build big things! Coral polyps, which live in the warm, **shallow** parts of the ocean, are probably the biggest builders on the planet. Each polyp uses calcium from seawater to build itself a hard limestone skeleton. When a polyp dies, its skeleton **remains**. Young polyps attach themselves to the old skeletons and make new skeletons. Over time, strange and wonderful shapes are slowly built up into amazing coral reefs.

B _____ Some coral reefs are huge, and the Great Barrier Reef in Australia is the largest of them all. It covers nearly 350,000 square kilometers.

C Scientists sometimes think of coral reefs as underwater cities. A quarter of all known ocean species live in and on reefs—there are nearly a thousand coral species. Reefs are also home to millions of sea creatures, like fish, crabs, turtles, and sharks.

D _____ Humans don't live in coral reef cities, but we benefit from them. Reefs create jobs for people in the fishing industry and other related businesses. They also supply us with food. Reefs protect our coasts—the coral slows down waves and protects beaches from erosion.

E Coral reefs are also **popular** with divers—many countries benefit from the tourists they **attract**. Finally, chemicals from reef creatures are used to create new medicines, which help doctors treat different illnesses.

F _____ Coral reefs are important, yet we don't take good care of them. About 20 percent of the world's reefs are already dead. Some experts **warn** that all reefs may be gone by 2050.

G Why are reefs in such trouble? For one thing, people catch too many reef fish and often **damage** the reefs—divers sometimes break off pieces of coral. Many people make and sell coral jewelry, too.

H Polluted water also causes problems because a certain type of algae grows in dirty water. This type of algae harms the reefs. Another type of algae is good for the reefs. But global warming is causing warmer ocean temperatures, which can cause polyps to lose this helpful algae. Without it, coral turns white. This is called "coral bleaching."

I _____ Can we save coral reefs? Experts say yes—if we make hard choices. More than 100 countries have created marine protected areas, where fishing is limited or banned. Another important step is fighting pollution.

J Humans and coral polyps are very different, but both build amazing cities. All of us will benefit if we protect our beautiful oceans.

COMPREHENSION

A Answer the questions about *Cities in the Sea*.

1 **PURPOSE** The main purpose of the article is to _____ .

   a identify the plants and animals that live in coral reefs

   b explain why coral reefs are important

   c tell readers about the Great Barrier Reef

2 **DETAIL** Coral reefs help protect coasts by _____ .

   a slowing down waves

   b releasing important chemicals

   c absorbing pollution

3 **DETAIL** What does the author say about the chemicals from reef creatures?

   a They damage the coral reefs.

   b They affect the algae growing near reefs.

   c They help scientists create new medicines.

4 **COHESION** The following sentence would best be placed at the end of which paragraph?

   If this process continues, the coral dies.

   a paragraph D   **b** paragraph F   **c** paragraph H

5 **INFERENCE** The helpful type of algae gives corals their _____ .

   a color   **b** hardness   **c** shape

IDIOM

If you think something is "fishy," you think it's _____ .
a amazing
b funny
c suspicious

B Complete the word web. Use words or phrases from the article.

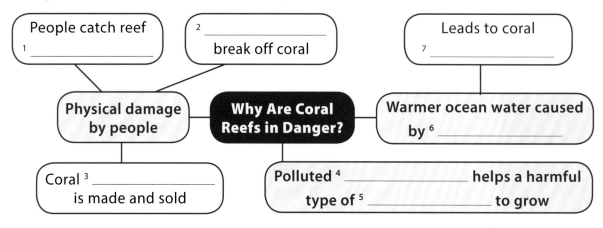

People catch reef 1 _____

2 _____ break off coral

Leads to coral 7 _____

Physical damage by people

Why Are Coral Reefs in Danger?

Warmer ocean water caused by 6 _____

Coral 3 _____ is made and sold

Polluted 4 _____ helps a harmful type of 5 _____ to grow

C CRITICAL THINKING Reflecting Talk with a partner. What kinds of "hard choices" do you think we need to make in order to save coral reefs?

VOCABULARY

A **Find the bold words below in the article.** Then circle the correct answers.

1 A lake that is **shallow** is *very big / not deep*.

2 If something **remains**, it *continues to exist / disappears*.

3 Things that are **popular** are enjoyed by *very few / many* people.

4 If something **attracts** people, it has features that cause people to *come to it / go away*.

5 When you **warn** someone about something, you tell them that something *good / bad* may happen.

6 When you **damage** an object, you *break or destroy / fix or improve* it.

B **Read the information below.** Then draw an arrow from the **bold** word or phrase to where it should go in each sentence (1–5).

> When we don't know the exact number or wish to be vague, we can use expressions to give approximate numbers:
>
> *about …*   *around …*   *more than …*   *nearly …*   *… or so*

1 The Great Barrier Reef covers an area of 350,000 square kilometers. **nearly**

2 It contributes 70,000 jobs to the Australian economy. **around**

3 It consists of 3,000 individual coral reefs. **about**

4 It's home to 1,500 species of fish. **more than**

5 The reef grows a centimeter each year. **or so**

WRITING

A **Read the email.**

B **What can the government do to help protect coral reefs?** Note some ideas.

C **Write a formal email using your notes from B.** Persuade a government official to help protect coral reefs in your country.

New message

To governmentofficial@mail.com

Subject Help protect coral reefs

Dear Sir or Madam,

I am writing about the state of our country's coral reefs. There are beautiful reefs near our beaches, which many tourists currently enjoy, but these reefs have suffered a lot of damage recently from fishermen and divers. I feel that we can protect our coral reefs by …

BONELESS **BEAUTIES**

Before You Watch

Take a quiz. What do you know about jellyfish? Circle **T** for true or **F** for false.

1	Jellyfish appeared on the Earth before dinosaurs.	T	F
2	Jellyfish are a type of fish.	T	F
3	Some jellyfish stings can kill a human.	T	F
4	Jellyfish have no hearts, blood, or brains.	T	F
5	A group of jellyfish can cover hundreds of square kilometers.	T	F

While You Watch

A ▶ 6.2 **Watch the video.** Check your answers to the quiz above. Is any of the information surprising?

B ▶ 6.2 **Watch again.** Circle the correct answers.

1 Another name for jellyfish is **sea jellies** / **jelly bells**.

2 The Australian box jellyfish is considered to be the **longest** / **most venomous** marine animal in the world.

3 Jellyfish are **60** / **95** percent water.

4 Groups of jellyfish—called **schools** / **blooms**—have been known to damage **ships** / **coral reefs**.

C **Look at these possible impacts of jellyfish.** Are they positive or negative? Or could they be both? Write **P** (positive), **N** (negative), or **B** (both). Then compare with a partner and discuss reasons for your answers.

1 Jellyfish use up much of the oxygen that farmed fish require. _____

2 Jellyfish provide shelter for younger fish that live within their tentacles. _____

3 Jellyfish are an additional food source for certain communities. _____

4 Jellyfish discourage tourism because beachgoers avoid going into the water. _____

5 Large groups of jellyfish block the water pipes of seaside power plants. _____

After You Watch

Talk with a partner. Look back at all the marine animals you have learned about in this unit. Which animal do you find most interesting? Why?

A **Complete the sentences.** Use the words in the box. Two words are extra.

> feathers   flippers   shells   tails   tusks

1 Oysters, mussels, and snails all live inside _____ .

2 Cats, dogs, and mice all have _____ .

3 An elephant has two _____ , but a narwhal has just one.

B **Rewrite these sentences.** Use *which* or *who.*

1 The sea otter lives along the Pacific coast. It uses rocks to break open shellfish.

   The sea otter, which uses rocks to break open shellfish,

   lives along the Pacific coast.

2 My teacher loves diving. She has a degree in oceanography.

   _____

   _____

3 Fur seals have large eyes. These allow them to see well underwater.

   _____

   _____

C **Correct the error in each sentence.**

         about six
1 We spent ~~six about~~ weeks at the research center.

2 He's 40 years around old.

3 We saw or so 30 fish while snorkeling.

4 There nearly are 20 people in the queue.

Sea nettle
jellyfish

SELF CHECK Now I can …

☐ talk about marine animals and their habitats

☐ add information about things and people

☐ discuss the importance of coral reefs

IT MIGHT HAVE BEEN
A TEMPLE

Ruins of an ancient
temple in Turkey

PREVIEW

A 🎧 **7.1 Listen.** Number these titles in order (1–3). One title is extra.

_____ Empty Homes

_____ Mysterious Bones Discovered

_____ The Legend of the Lost Gold

_____ Religion in the Ancient World

B 🎧 **7.1 Listen again.** What is the mystery in each story? Circle **a** or **b**.

1　**a** Where is the Inca king buried?

　　b Where is the lost treasure of the Inca?

2　**a** Why did the Anasazi suddenly leave their homes?

　　b How did the Anasazi build their multi-story homes?

3　**a** How old are the temple ruins?

　　b Which came first—religion or cities?

C **Talk with a partner.** Of the stories above, which do you find most interesting? Why?

> I find the story about the Anasazi most interesting because …

> I think the most interesting story is …

HISTORY AND CULTURE

UNIT GOALS

- talk about ancient and modern-day mysteries
- learn language for describing probability
- learn about ancient civilizations

LANGUAGE FOCUS

A 🎧 **7.2** **Listen and read.** What does Nadine think the item is? Then repeat the conversation and replace the words in **bold**.

REAL ENGLISH   What on earth … ?

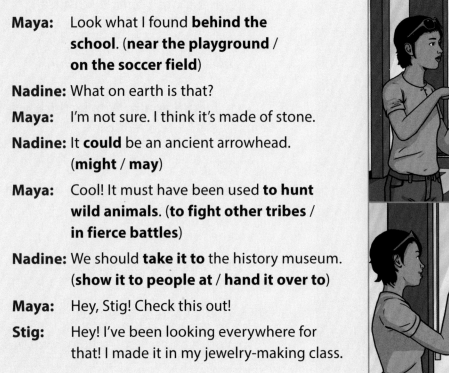

Maya: Look what I found **behind the school**. (**near the playground / on the soccer field**)

Nadine: What on earth is that?

Maya: I'm not sure. I think it's made of stone.

Nadine: It **could** be an ancient arrowhead. (**might / may**)

Maya: Cool! It must have been used **to hunt wild animals**. (**to fight other tribes / in fierce battles**)

Nadine: We should **take it to** the history museum. (**show it to people at / hand it over to**)

Maya: Hey, Stig! Check this out!

Stig: Hey! I've been looking everywhere for that! I made it in my jewelry-making class.

B 🎧 **7.3** **Look at the chart.** Then circle the correct answers below.

DESCRIBING PROBABILITY (USING MODALS OF PROBABILITY)		
	Less Sure	**More Sure**
Present	The lost treasure **could/might** be in a cave. But the treasure **might not** even exist.	The jewels **can't** be in that cave—it's too high. This gold necklace **must** be valuable. No one's ever found the treasure. It **must not** exist.
Past	This house **could/might** have belonged to the royal family. However, it **might not** have belonged to an important person.	The house is huge, so it **must** have belonged to the royal family. There are bedrooms in the building, so it **couldn't** have been a school.

1 If we use modal + *be*, we are referring to the **past / present**.

2 If we use modal + *have been*, we are referring to the **past / present**.

3 We use *could* or *might* when we are **less / more** sure of something, and *must* or *can't* when we are **less / more** sure.

C 🎧 **7.4** **Complete the conversations.** Circle the correct words. Then listen and check your answers.

1 **Mary:** This building is very old. What do you think it was used for?

   Greg: I'm not sure. It ¹ **might** / **must** have been a temple. What do you think?

   Mary: No, it ² **couldn't** / **might not** have been a temple because there's already one right next to it. They wouldn't have built two temples so close together.

2 **Yasmin:** Whose notebook is this?

   Karl: I have no idea. It ³ **might** / **must** be Jessie's.

   Yasmin: Oh, wait—here's a photo of a puppy. It ⁴ **must have belonged** / **must belong** to Laura. She just got a puppy last month.

D **Rewrite these sentences.** Use the words in parentheses.

1 It's possible that the treasure is at the bottom of the lake. (**could**)

   The treasure _could be at the bottom of the lake_ .

2 I'm certain that this item is thousands of years old. (**must**)

   This item _____ .

3 It's possible that he didn't call his parents. (**might not**)

   He _____ .

4 She definitely got home before midnight. (**must**)

   She _____ .

5 We're certain that the teacher isn't over 40 years old. (**can't**)

   The teacher _____ .

E **Work with a partner. Student A:** Turn to page 150. **Student B:** Turn to page 153. Take turns reading each mystery. Discuss what you think happened.

A stone ball from Costa Rica

The stone balls might have been part of a religious ceremony.

Maybe. Or they could have been used in games.

RAPA NUI

Moai statues on Easter Island, Chile

A ▶7.1 **Watch the video.** Check (✓) the topics discussed.

- ☐ when the island of Rapa Nui was discovered
- ☐ the height and weight of the *moai* statues
- ☐ how the *moai* may have been moved around the island
- ☐ where to get the best view of the *moai*
- ☐ theories about the purpose of the *moai*

B ▶7.1 **Watch again.** Circle the correct answers.

1 There are nearly **500** / **900** *moai* on Rapa Nui.

2 The early Rapa Nui people probably used **ropes** / **animals** to move the statues.

3 Most *moai* **face inland** / **look out to sea**.

4 One theory about the *moai* is that they **helped scare away enemies** / **represented political leaders**.

DO YOU KNOW?

The Statue of Unity, which is the tallest statue in the world, is located in _____ .
a India
b Japan
c Dubai

C Work in groups. Rapa Nui has seen a big increase in tourism in the past few years, as many people come to see the *moai*. What are some pros and cons of this? Complete the chart.

Pros	Cons

D CRITICAL THINKING Reflecting **Talk with a partner.** Based on your notes in **C**, would you want to visit Rapa Nui? Does the mystery of the *moai* make you want to see the statues for yourself?

PROJECT Go online. Choose one of these ancient structures and learn about the mystery surrounding it. Share your findings with a partner.
- Stonehenge
- Machu Picchu
- The Yonaguni Monument

PRONUNCIATION review: reduction of *have*

🎧 7.5 **Listen.** Write the words you hear. Then listen again and repeat the sentences.

1 The effort to construct the statues _____ considerable.

2 The heavy statues _____ easy to move.

3 The Rapa Nui people _____ the statues for religious purposes.

COMMUNICATION

Solve a puzzle. Work in groups. You are on a quest to find treasure from different civilizations. There are three chests, each containing an item from a certain culture. Each chest is in a different place. Use the clues to complete the chart below.

CULTURES
Aztec, Inca, Maya

ITEMS
mask, cup, bowl

PLACES
mountain, cave, jungle

CLUES
The Maya chest is one number smaller than the Inca chest.

The Aztec chest can't be Chest 1, but it must contain the cup.

Chest 2 is in a cave.

Chest 1 contains the bowl, but it isn't in the jungle.

CHEST	CULTURE	ITEM	PLACE
1			
2			
3			

The Maya chest could be Chest 1 or 2.

READING

A **Look at the title and the photo.** What do you know about the Maya? When and where did they live?

B **Scan the article.** Underline the two cities mentioned.

C **Skim the article.** What did archeologists use to think happened to the Maya? What do they think now?

Mayan ruins in
Tikal, Guatemala

MAYA MYSTERY

By Guy Gugliotta, writing for *National Geographic*

A 🎧 7.6 A lost world is hidden in the rain forests of Central America. There, the ancient Maya built huge, incredible cities. The Maya civilization was at its **peak** for 650 years, but about a thousand years ago, the cities were suddenly **abandoned**. Today, trees and plants cover the buildings, and many temples are now ruins. What happened? Why did the Maya leave their cities?

B For years, archeologists thought that a disaster, like a volcano or an earthquake, must have hit the Maya. Diseases, which were brought by invaders, might have spread quickly through the **population**. However, researchers now think the Maya had a lot of different problems, leading to their disappearance.

C To understand what happened to the Maya, *National Geographic* sent me to Central America. I visited Mayan cities and talked to archeologists who are studying them.

D One hot day, I stood next to a river near the ruins of Cancuén. It used to be a great city, but everything changed 1,200 years ago. Invaders came suddenly—probably by boat. I pictured them as I looked at the river. In my mind, I saw the invaders fighting the soldiers—first at the river, and then in the town.

E I followed the path that the invaders must have taken, which led to the ruins of a large pool. The pool once provided drinking water for the city. The invaders killed the city's leaders and threw their bodies into the water. They killed the king and queen, too, and buried them nearby.

F The invaders then left, taking nothing of value. No one knows who they were, what they wanted, or where they went. Experts think that the city's remaining population escaped into the rain forest.

G I learned a different story in Tikal, one of the greatest Mayan cities. Thirteen hundred years ago, over 50,000 people lived there. The city had about 3,000 major buildings. But, like Cancuén, its people left.

H Archeologists think Tikal might have had a drought. The **lack of** rain would have made it hard to grow food. War with neighboring cities might also have made Tikal weak. The Maya believed that their leaders were gods, so when the king couldn't bring rain or protect them, people started to question his power. Their community might then have **collapsed**.

I Walking among the temples at Tikal, I **imagined** the people living there in the city's last days. I could picture them hungry, tired, and scared. Like the Maya in Cancuén, they left behind a great city and a great mystery.

COMPREHENSION

A Answer the questions about *Maya Mystery*.

1 **MAIN IDEA** What is the mystery in the title?

   a Why did the Maya civilization disappear?

   b Who were the Maya people?

   c Where did the Maya hide their treasure?

2 **INFERENCE** The archeologists thought the Maya probably died from a natural disaster or a disease because _____.

   a they disappeared so suddenly

   b the Maya had a lot of enemies

   c they were bad at farming

3 **COHESION** Where is the best place for this sentence in paragraph E?

   Then it became a tomb for the local leaders.

   a after sentence 1   b after sentence 2   c after sentence 4

4 **DETAIL** Why did invaders attack Cancuén?

   a to take their treasure   b to take over the city   c no one knows

5 **DETAIL** What is known to be true about Cancuén but not Tikal?

   a Its people left the city.

   b Its people believed in gods.

   c Its rulers were killed by invaders.

B Read the sentences below. Circle **Fa** for fact or **Th** for theory.

1 The ancient Maya built huge cities in Central America.   **Fa   Th**

2 The Maya population was affected by a natural disaster.   **Fa   Th**

3 There is a river near the ruins of Cancuén.   **Fa   Th**

4 The people who invaded Cancuén came by boat.   **Fa   Th**

5 Tikal experienced a drought, which made it hard to grow food.   **Fa   Th**

C **CRITICAL THINKING Ranking** Which of these ancient civilizations would you like to go back and live in? Rank them from **1** (most like to live in) to **4** (least like to live in). Then share your ranking and reasons with a partner.

_____ Maya   _____ Rapa Nui   _____ Egypt   _____ China

VOCABULARY

A **Find the bold words below in the article.** Then circle the correct answers.

1 A civilization at its **peak** is at its *weakest / strongest*.

2 If people **abandon** a city, they *invade / leave* it.

3 A country's **population** is the number of *people / buildings* there.

4 A **lack of** water means there's *not enough / too much* water.

5 When a civilization **collapses**, it *continues to be successful / is unable to continue*.

6 If you **imagine** something, you *try to forget about it / form a picture of it in your mind*.

B **Read the information below.** Then add the examples to the correct column in the chart. What other natural disasters can you name? Which occur in your country?

> Below are some examples of natural disasters. Use a dictionary to check their meanings.
>
> avalanche   blizzard   flood   hurricane   tsunami

They involve water	They involve snow

WRITING

A Read the paragraph.

B **What mysteries do you know of?** Choose one and make notes about it.

C **Write a short essay.** Describe the mystery. Use your notes from **B** to help you.

CROP FORMATIONS

Every year, mysterious crop circles or formations appear in fields in England. Some people think aliens might have made them. Others think that people made them as a prank ...

THE *LOST COLONY*

Before You Watch

Talk with a partner. What challenges do you think the early English settlers in the New World (i.e., the Americas) faced?

While You Watch

A ▶ 7.2 **Watch Part 1 of the video.** Which expedition(s) do the statements below relate to? Check (✓) the correct columns.

	Expedition 1	Expedition 2	Expedition 3
It returned to England.			
The colonists disappeared.			
A map of Roanoke was created.			
It arrived at Roanoke in 1587.			
A child was born in the colony.			

B ▶ 7.3 **Watch Part 2 of the video.** What theories about the colonists' disappearance are mentioned? Circle the correct answers.

1 The colonists moved to **Croatoan Island** / **an island near Croatoan**.

2 The colonists **tried to return to England** / **moved farther inland**.

3 The colonists died from disease or **an earthquake** / **drought**.

4 The colonists were killed by **Native Americans** / **wild animals**.

C. **Work with a partner.** Of the theories in **B**, which do you think is most likely? Which is least likely? Can you think of any other possible explanations?

After You Watch

Talk with a partner. The mystery of the Roanoke colony has been adapted into a TV show. Would you like to watch it? Why or why not?

An actress portraying Eleanor Dare, the governor's daughter

A Complete the sentences. Use the words in parentheses. In each set, one word is extra.

1 In many early _____ , people _____ the land and practiced _____ . (*civilizations*, *collapsed*, *farmed*, *religion*)

2 When the _____ finally _____ the king, they took all his _____ . (*built*, *captured*, *invaders*, *treasure*)

3 Written _____ have helped _____ solve the _____ . (*archeologists*, *mystery*, *records*, *ruins*)

B Complete the conversations. Circle the correct answers.

1 **A:** Do you think the early Rapa Nui people died from disease?

  B: Definitely. Disease **must play** / **must have played** a big part.

2 **A:** Do you know where my jacket is?

  B: It **could** / **mustn't** be in the dining room. Have you looked there?

3 **A:** Whose backpack is this? Is it Ken's?

  B: It **might** / **can't** be his. His is blue—this one is black.

C Complete the sentences. Use the words in the box. One word is extra.

avalanche	flood	hurricane	tsunami

1 After a week of rain, the river overflowed and caused a(n) _____ .

2 We fear that the sudden _____ may have buried the skiers in the mountains.

3 A huge earthquake caused _____ warnings across the Pacific.

SELF CHECK Now I can …

☐ talk about ancient and modern-day mysteries

☐ use language for describing probability

☐ talk about ancient civilizations

IT'S TALLER THAN THE EIFFEL TOWER!

The minute hand of the Mecca clock is 23 meters long.

PREVIEW

A 🎧 **8.1 Listen.** Match each structure (**1–4**) with the correct country. One country is extra.

1 Arsenalna Station ○   ○ Japan

2 Seikan Tunnel ○   ○ Egypt

3 F&F Tower ○   ○ Ukraine

4 Abraj Al-Bait ○   ○ Panama

                    ○ Saudi Arabia

B 🎧 **8.1 Listen again.** Complete the sentences. Use the correct form of the words in the box. One word is extra.

> deep   interesting   long   old   tall

1 Arsenalna Station is the _____ subway station in the world.

2 The Seikan Tunnel is the world's _____ tunnel with an undersea section.

3 The F&F Tower, which looks like a giant screw, is one of the _____ buildings in the world.

4 The Abraj Al-Bait complex has the world's _____ clock tower.

C Talk with a partner. Which of the structures above would you most like to see? Why?

PEOPLE AND PLACES

UNIT GOALS

- talk about architectural and engineering wonders
- learn language for describing and comparing things
- learn about an extreme railway journey in Africa

LANGUAGE FOCUS

A 🎧 **8.2** **Listen and read.** Why can't Ming and Stig see much from the top of the skyscraper? Then repeat the conversation and replace the words in **bold**.

> **REAL ENGLISH** What a shame!

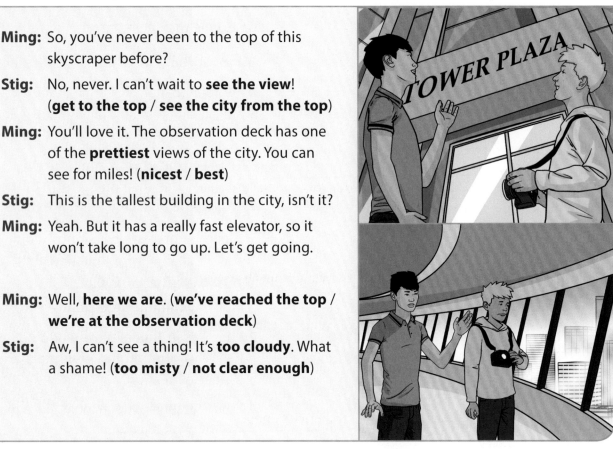

Ming: So, you've never been to the top of this skyscraper before?

Stig: No, never. I can't wait to **see the view**! (**get to the top / see the city from the top**)

Ming: You'll love it. The observation deck has one of the **prettiest** views of the city. You can see for miles! (**nicest / best**)

Stig: This is the tallest building in the city, isn't it?

Ming: Yeah. But it has a really fast elevator, so it won't take long to go up. Let's get going.

Ming: Well, **here we are**. (**we've reached the top / we're at the observation deck**)

Stig: Aw, I can't see a thing! It's **too cloudy**. What a shame! (**too misty / not clear enough**)

B 🎧 **8.3** **Look at the chart.** Then circle the correct answers below.

DESCRIBING AND COMPARING THINGS (USING *TOO*, *ENOUGH*, COMPARATIVE/ SUPERLATIVE ADJECTIVES)
You can't get to Arsenalna Station on just one escalator. It's **too deep**.
Celia is **old enough** to drive. But Max is only 14, so he is**n't old enough** to drive.
Elevator 1 is just **as fast as** Elevator 2. But it's **not as large as** Elevator 2.
The new hotel is **taller than** the clock tower. It was **more expensive** to build **than** the mall.
The castle is **the oldest** building in the city. It's also **the most popular** tourist attraction.

1 We use *too* + adjective to say something is **less or more than necessary** / **the necessary amount**.

2 We use adjective + *enough* to say something is **less than the necessary amount** / **the necessary amount**.

3 We use *as* + adjective + *as* to say two things are **equal** / **not equal**.

C **Complete the sentences.** Use the words in the box. Add *too* or *enough*.

expensive	hungry	slow	tall	wide

1 I can't afford the ticket price to the observation deck. It's _____.

2 Six cars can't drive side by side on that bridge. It's not _____.

3 This train is _____. We'll never get to the theater in time.

4 I'm not _____ to reach the top shelf. Can you help me?

5 Sorry, but I already ate. I was _____ to wait!

D 🎧 8.4 **Complete the information.** Use the correct form of the adjectives in parentheses. Add *the* or *as* if necessary. Then listen and check your answers.

1 <u>The most memorable</u> (**memorable**) way to see New York City is from one of its many skyscrapers.

2 _____ (**famous**) is surely the Empire State Building. But some visitors who have gone to Top of the Rock at Rockefeller Center say the view from there is just 3 _____ (**good**) the view from the Empire State Building. Others even claim that the view is actually 4 _____ (**good**) in the whole city. Tickets, however, are just 5 _____ (**expensive**) those for the Empire State Building, so you don't save any money. But Top of the Rock's lines are 6 _____ (**short**), and its elevator is 7 _____ (**fast**). So while Top of the Rock is not 8 _____ (**famous**) the Empire State Building, it's attracting more and more tourists.

E **Work in pairs.** Complete the questions below. Use the correct form of the adjectives in parentheses, and add *the* or *than* if necessary. Then take turns asking and answering the questions with your partner. Ask follow-up questions to get additional information.

1 What's _____ (**hot**) place you've ever been to?

2 Who's _____ (**interesting**) person you know?

3 Which animal is _____ (**intelligent**)—a dolphin or a dog?

4 Is it better to have a sibling who's _____ (**old**) or _____ (**young**) you?

5 What's _____ (**good**) present you've ever received?

6 What's _____ (**scary**) movie you've ever seen?

THE WORLD'S LONGEST FOOTBRIDGE

Charles Kuonen Suspension Bridge, Switzerland

A ▶ 8.1 **Watch the video.** Circle **T** for true or **F** for false.

1	It takes an hour to cross the bridge.	T	F
2	The bridge replaced an older bridge.	T	F
3	The bridge was designed so it would not swing.	T	F
4	The bridge is open all year long.	T	F

B ▶ 8.1 **Watch again.** Complete the notes about the bridge with numbers from the box. Two numbers are extra.

10	28	65	85	250	494	2017

1 Length: _____ meters

2 Highest point: _____ meters above ground

3 Time it took to build: _____ weeks

4 Width: _____ centimeters

5 Maximum number of hikers on the bridge: _____

DO YOU KNOW?

Nutty Narrows Bridge, the world's narrowest bridge, allows _____ to cross above the road.
a koalas
b squirrels
c monkeys

C Complete the information below. Circle the correct answers.

The United Arab Emirates is the proud holder of many world records. For example, Dubai is home to the world's [1] **taller** / **tallest** building, the Burj Khalifa. A mosque in Abu Dhabi has the [2] **largest** / **most large** hand-woven carpet in the world. And in Ras al-Khaimah—about 45 minutes from Dubai—people can take a ride on the world's [3] **long enough** / **longest** zipline. Riders zoom down from a mountaintop 1,680 meters above sea level, reaching speeds of up to 150 kilometers per hour. The zipline is 2.83 kilometers long—that's [4] **longer than** / **too long** 28 soccer fields! Would you be [5] **as brave as** / **brave enough** to take a ride on this zipline?

D CRITICAL THINKING Comparing Talk with a partner. Would you rather walk across the Charles Kuonen Suspension Bridge or ride the zipline in Ras al-Khaimah? Why?

PROJECT Go online. Find another example of a famous tourist attraction. Make some notes about it and share with a partner.

PRONUNCIATION emphatic stress

🎧 8.5 **Listen.** Underline the word in each sentence that receives the most stress. Then listen again and repeat the sentences.

1 The bridge is only 65 centimeters wide.

2 The walk across the bridge is way too scary for me.

3 We didn't spend nearly enough time in the Alps.

4 The views were much more beautiful than I expected.

COMMUNICATION

Create a quiz. Work with a partner. Complete these sentences to create a true/false quiz. Then test your quiz on another pair.

1 _____ is the biggest _____ in the world.

2 _____ is taller than _____.

3 _____ is not as long as _____.

4 _____ is faster than _____.

5 _____ has a smaller population than _____.

6 _____ is the oldest _____.

Dubai International Airport is the biggest airport in the world. True or false?

READING

A Scan the article. In which country does the Iron Ore Train operate? What is the main purpose of this train?

B Skim the article. Underline all the adjectives that describe the train journey.

C Talk with a partner. The Iron Ore Train doesn't charge people who ride on it. Why do you think this is?

THE IRON ORE TRAIN

A 🎧 8.6 As the sun starts to set, a group of people stand by the rail track near the village of Choum, deep in the Sahara Desert. They pass around water and move into position. Suddenly, bright lights appear in the distance and a train comes into view. When it arrives for a five-minute stop, people pull themselves up to the top of the train cars. They have just **boarded** what has been called "the world's most extreme railway."

B Here, in a remote corner of the West African country of Mauritania, is the Iron Ore Train. Opened in 1963, the train runs every day from the mining town of Zouérat to the port of Nouadhibou, then back again. Its main purpose is to bring iron ore—the country's biggest **export**—from the mines. Consisting of more than 200 cars, the train is about 2.5 kilometers in length and can **transport** 17,000 tons of iron ore. It's one of the longest trains in the world.

Passengers on the Iron Ore Train
(photographed by Daniel Rodrigues)

C There are few roads in this **region** of the Sahara, so the railway is one of the few ways to get across the desert. For many Mauritanians, it is the only way to reach places deep in the Sahara. They **rely on** the train for many things: to see family, to sell their **goods**, and to search for work. They pass the time by chatting and sipping tea.

D It is by no means an easy ride. The journey—which can take anywhere from 16 to 21 hours traveling one-way—is dirty and uncomfortable. Passengers wrap their faces in scarves to protect themselves from the hot desert winds and the iron ore dust. Temperatures can exceed 40°C during the day, and it gets very cold at night. Sandstorms are frequent, the ride is bumpy, and death from falling is not uncommon.

E But for some tourists, a trip on the Iron Ore Train is the adventure of a lifetime. It requires no reservations, no tickets, and no cash. There is little to do but enjoy the incredible landscape and make friends with the locals.

F For photographer Daniel Rodrigues, who made the trip and took photographs of his experience, it was the night sky that he remembers the most. "Only in the desert can you see this," he said. "Millions and millions of stars."

COMPREHENSION

IDIOM

If everything is going well in your life, you are _____.
a off the rails
b on the right track

A Answer the questions about *The Iron Ore Train*.

1 **DETAIL** Which statement about the Iron Ore Train is true?

   a It has been operating since the 1940s.

   b A round-trip journey could take about 40 hours.

   c No one has ever fallen off the train and died.

2 **INFERENCE** What kind of traveler would probably be most interested in taking a trip on this train?

   a someone who is most comfortable traveling in cities

   b someone who likes to go on adventure trips

   c someone who enjoys taking group tour packages

3 **PURPOSE** What is the purpose of paragraph C?

   a to make the train ride sound enjoyable to the reader

   b to describe what life would be like without the train

   c to explain why the train is important to local people

4 **VOCABULARY** The phrase *by no means* in paragraph D can be replaced with _____.

   a not at all   b expected to be   c in some ways

5 **DETAIL** What should a tourist do if they want to ride the train?

   a make a reservation

   b ask a local to help them buy a ticket

   c just jump on when it stops

B Match each paragraph with the information it contains.

1 Paragraph A ○   ○ statistics about the train

2 Paragraph B ○   ○ a quote from a photographer who took the train

3 Paragraph C ○   ○ reasons why the train journey can be unpleasant

4 Paragraph D ○   ○ reasons why some tourists take the train

5 Paragraph E ○   ○ reasons why locals take the train

6 Paragraph F ○   ○ a description of how people get on the train

C CRITICAL THINKING Reflecting Talk with a partner. Would you be interested in taking a trip on the Iron Ore Train? Why or why not?

VOCABULARY

A **Find the bold words below in the article.** Then circle the correct answers.

1 If you **board** a train, you get *on* / *off* it.

2 **Exports** are things that are *bought from* / *sold to* another country.

3 *Cars and trucks* / *Phones and laptops* are used to **transport** people and things.

4 A particular **region** of a country refers to *its official language* / *an area of land*.

5 If you **rely on** something, you *need* / *don't need* it.

6 **Goods** refer to *physical items* / *people's feelings*.

B **Read the information below.** Then complete the word web about travel using the words in the box. Can you think of other examples to add to the word web? Tell a partner.

> A word web is one way to organize vocabulary around a topic. You can add more words to it as you learn them.

car   first-class   journey   luggage   passengers
passport   plane   round-trip   tourists   trip

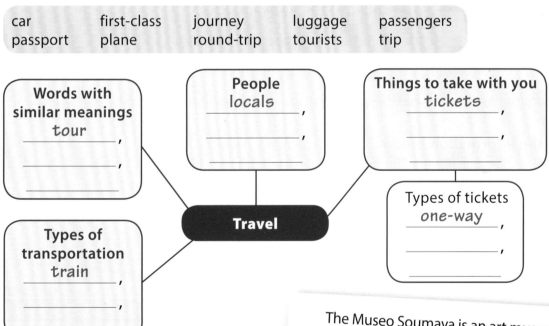

Words with similar meanings
tour _____ ,
_____ ,
_____

People
locals _____ ,
_____ ,

Things to take with you
tickets _____ ,
_____ ,

Types of tickets
one-way _____ ,
_____ ,
_____

Types of transportation
train _____ ,
_____ ,

Travel

WRITING

A **Read the paragraph.**

B **Choose an interesting human-made structure.** Make notes about it.

C **Write about the structure.** Say why it's impressive.

The Museo Soumaya is an art museum in Mexico City. It's one of the most famous buildings in Mexico. Opened in 2011, it was designed by the architect Fernando Romero. The outside of the building is covered in tiles …

THE *GREEN* MUSEUM

Before You Watch

Talk with a partner. Look at the photo. What do you think makes this museum "green"?

While You Watch

A   ▶ 8.2   **Watch the video.** Check (✓) four things you can find at the California Academy of Sciences.

- ☐ a research center
- ☐ a rain forest
- ☐ a playground
- ☐ a flower market
- ☐ an aquarium
- ☐ a coral reef

B   ▶ 8.2   **Watch again.** Circle the correct answers.

1   The California Academy of Sciences has the **biggest / oldest** green museum in the world.

2   The climate in the dome is **cool and dry / hot and humid**.

3   The team's goal is to make the exhibits more **accessible / lifelike**.

4   The water in the aquarium comes from **a human-made lake / the ocean**.

5   The aquarium has the **deepest / widest** tank for a coral reef in the world.

C   **Complete the information below.** Circle the correct answers.

The California Academy of Sciences also houses the Morrison Planetarium. Known for its 23-meter-diameter screen, the planetarium offers a fully immersive viewing experience. Its show called *Passport to the Universe*, [1] **which / who** is narrated by the actor Tom Hanks, [2] **describes / has been described** as being "[3] **too exciting / as exciting as** anything in a theme park." Every star a viewer sees in the planetarium mirrors a real-world star, making this one of the [4] **accurate / most accurate** digital universes ever created.

After You Watch

Talk with a partner. What is the most interesting museum you have visited? What made it so interesting?

A **Complete the sentences.** Use the adjectives in the box. One adjective is extra.

> expensive   fast   hungry   old   tall

1 Why do we have so many _____ buildings? They block out the sun!

2 A Banksy painting sold for more than $12 million in 2019. That's really _____ .

3 The McLaren F1 is a super _____ car—it can reach speeds of up to 386 kilometers per hour.

4 The Ponte Sant'Angelo bridge in Rome is very _____ . It was built around A.D. 134.

B **Correct the error in each sentence.**

1 I think James is older ~~as~~ *than* Barbara.

2 Jennifer is just as prettier as her sister.

3 Eduardo is to young to go on the roller coaster.

4 Aaron is the more talented person I know.

5 Eun-joo is finally enough old to vote.

The dome in the California Academy of Sciences, San Francisco

C **Complete the sentences.** Use words from the word web on page 99.

1 Where did you park your _____ ?

2 How many country stamps do you have in your _____ ?

3 You can collect your _____ at the Baggage Claim area.

4 Have you ever flown _____ ? I hear it's very expensive.

SELF CHECK   Now I can …

☐ talk about architectural and engineering wonders

☐ use language for describing and comparing things

☐ describe an extreme railway journey in Africa

HE'S A
GREAT
ACTOR,
ISN'T HE?

Chris Hemsworth on the set of *Thor: The Dark World*

PREVIEW

A 🎧 **9.1 Listen to four conversations about different movies and TV shows.** Does each person want to watch the movie or TV show again? Write **Y** (yes) or **N** (no).

1 Megan _____   3 Ling _____

2 Junko _____   4 Terry _____

B 🎧 **9.1 Listen again.** Circle the correct answers.

1 Megan thinks the plot of the first *Thor* movie was very **interesting** / **dull**.

2 Junko says the costumes in *Beauty and the Beast* are **gorgeous** / **quite plain**.

3 Ling thinks *Frozen 2* is a bit **predictable** / **overrated**, but she likes the soundtrack.

4 Terry says the acting in *Stranger Things* is **unrealistic** / **superb**.

C Talk with a partner. Describe a recent movie or TV show you have seen. Share what you liked or didn't like about it.

> I saw the new *Wonder Woman* movie recently. The story was pretty exciting!

> How was the acting?

HISTORY AND CULTURE

UNIT GOALS

- talk about what makes movies successful or unsuccessful

- use language to ask for confirmation or information

- learn about why people enjoy feeling scared

LANGUAGE FOCUS

A 🎧9.2 **Listen and read.** What don't Nadine and Maya want to miss? Then repeat the conversation and replace the words in **bold**.

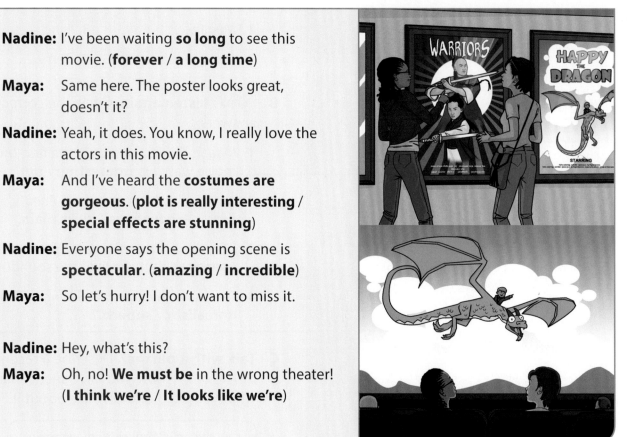

Nadine: I've been waiting **so long** to see this movie. (**forever** / **a long time**)

Maya: Same here. The poster looks great, doesn't it?

Nadine: Yeah, it does. You know, I really love the actors in this movie.

Maya: And I've heard the **costumes are gorgeous**. (**plot is really interesting** / **special effects are stunning**)

Nadine: Everyone says the opening scene is **spectacular**. (**amazing** / **incredible**)

Maya: So let's hurry! I don't want to miss it.

Nadine: Hey, what's this?

Maya: Oh, no! **We must be** in the wrong theater! (**I think we're** / **It looks like we're**)

B 🎧9.3 **Look at the chart.** Then circle the correct answers below.

ASKING FOR CONFIRMATION OR INFORMATION (USING TAG QUESTIONS)	
Leonardo DiCaprio **is** a good actor, **isn't he**?	Yes, he is.
That TV show **was** amazing, **wasn't it**?	Yes, it was.
You **liked** the ending of the movie, **didn't you**?	Yeah, I did.
You **haven't** been to the new movie theater, **have you**?	No, I haven't.
Meryl Streep **will** star in a new TV series next year, **won't she**?	Actually, she won't.
You **can't** see that movie until you're 18, **can you**?	No, I can't.

1 We use tag questions when we expect the listener to **agree** / **disagree** with us.

2 When a statement is in the affirmative, the question tag is in the **affirmative** / **negative**.

3 When a statement is in the negative, the question tag is in the **affirmative** / **negative**.

C Complete the tag questions. Then ask and answer the questions with a partner.

1 Special effects make movies more exciting, ___*don't they*___ ?

2 You didn't watch TV last night, _____ ?

3 You haven't seen every *Star Wars* movie, _____ ?

4 Most romantic comedies are really predictable, _____ ?

5 You don't like action movies very much, _____ ?

6 You're not a fan of superhero movies, _____ ?

D 🎧 9.4 Complete the conversation. Write appropriate tag forms and answers. Then listen and check.

Sam: Do you like the actress Scarlett Johansson?

Kylie: She was in the *Avengers* movies, [1] _____ ?

Sam: Yes, [2] _____ . She played Black Widow.

Kylie: Yeah, I think she's really talented. By the way, I'm taking my nephew out for a movie tomorrow. Do you have any suggestions?

Sam: Hmm … He likes animated movies, [3] _____ ?

Kylie: Yeah, [4] _____ . What do you have in mind?

Sam: How about the latest *Lego* movie? He hasn't seen that yet, [5] _____ ?

Kylie: I don't think so. Maybe we'll watch that. Thanks for the suggestion.

E Work in groups. Talk about the topics below. Ask follow-up questions.

| favorite actors/actresses | action movies | movie soundtracks | animated movies |
| science fiction movies | favorite books | new TV shows | pop music |

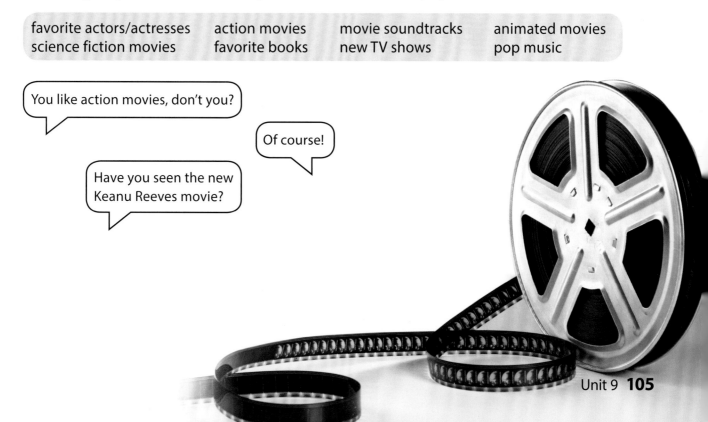

You like action movies, don't you?

Of course!

Have you seen the new Keanu Reeves movie?

MOVIE FLOPS

DISNEP A WRINKLE IN TIME

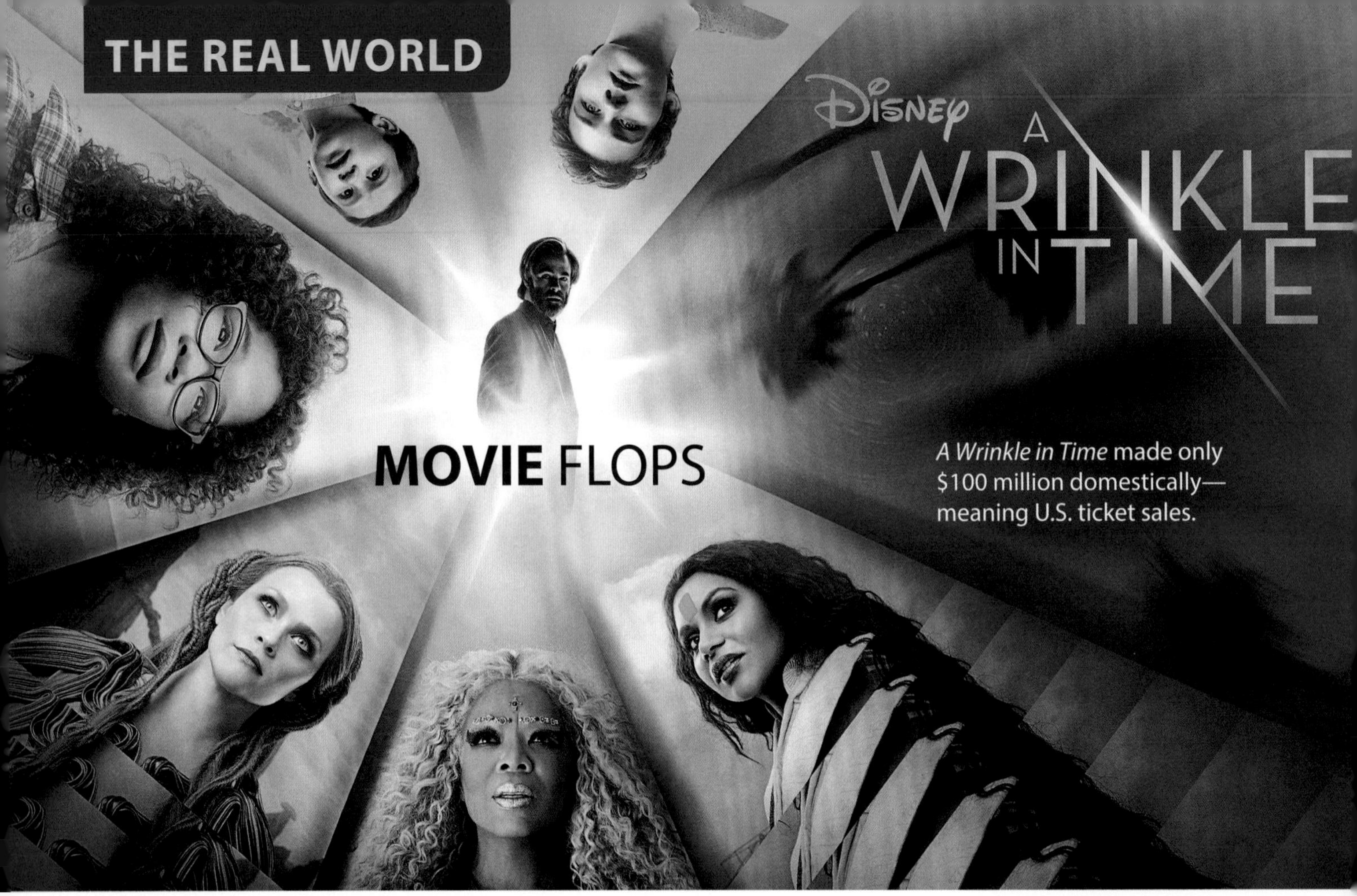

A Wrinkle in Time made only $100 million domestically—meaning U.S. ticket sales.

A ▶ 9.1 **Watch the video.** Circle **T** for true or **F** for false.

1	The movie *Mortal Engines* is considered a flop.	**T**	**F**
2	The movie *Warcraft* did poorly outside of North America.	**T**	**F**
3	*Blade Runner* was a big success when it was first released.	**T**	**F**

DO YOU KNOW?

A movie that's a massive hit is a

_____.

a double feature
b blockbuster
c midnight movie

B ▶ 9.1 **Watch again.** Match each movie with the reason it flopped.

1 *Treasure Planet* ○ ○ a miscast actor/actress
2 *John Carter* ○ ○ poor timing
3 *Aloha* ○ ○ poor marketing
4 *A Wrinkle in Time* ○ ○ bad reviews

C **Look at the chart below.** Based on the definition in the video, which of these movies are flops? Circle the movie titles.

Movie	Production cost	North America ticket sales	International ticket sales
Tomb Raider (2018)	$94 million	$58 million	$216 million
Robin Hood (2018)	$100 million	$30 million	$54 million
Blade Runner 2049 (2017)	$150 million	$92 million	$168 million
King Arthur (2017)	$175 million	$39 million	$107 million

D **CRITICAL THINKING** **Speculating** **Talk with a partner.** Read these "pitches" for possible movies. Which do you think is most likely to succeed? Which is most likely to flop? Why?

> Make *Black Panther* into an animated movie. Add some talking animals and a few musical numbers.

> Make a drama about *Genghis Khan*. Include big battle scenes. Cast *Leonardo DiCaprio* as Khan.

> Make a sequel to the movie *Titanic*. Cast Kate Winslet as Rose again. Show her life after the shipwreck.

PROJECT Think of a movie you like that generally did poorly. Find out how much money it lost. Why did it flop? What did you like about it?

PRONUNCIATION intonation in tag questions

A 🎧 **9.5** **Listen and repeat.**

1 That actor is really overrated, isn't he? (asking for confirmation)

2 You don't like movie sequels, do you? (asking for information)

B 🎧 **9.6** **Listen.** Mark each question tag with the intonation pattern ↗ or ↘. Then listen again and repeat the questions.

1 That film was awesome, wasn't it?

2 Anime comes from Japan, doesn't it?

3 You don't like 3D movies, do you?

4 Movie tickets are so expensive, aren't they?

COMMUNICATION

A **Look at the sentences below.** Write the name of a classmate in each blank that you think makes the sentence true.

1 _____ doesn't like romantic comedies.

2 _____ watches a lot of shows on Netflix.

3 _____ enjoys reading comic books.

4 _____ didn't play any video games last week.

5 _____ has never seen the movie *Titanic*.

B **Talk to the people in A.** Check your predictions using tag questions.

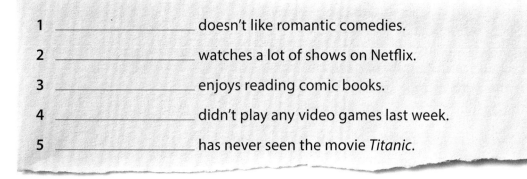

> You don't like romantic comedies, do you?

> No, I don't. / Actually, I do.

READING

A **Read the title.** What question do you think the article answers?
  a   Are horror movies less scary these days?
  b   Why do people watch horror movies?
  c   What are the best horror movies of all time?

B **Skim the article.** Add these headings (1–4) to the correct places. One heading is extra.
  1   A Brief History of Horror in Cinema
  2   The Biology of Fear
  3   Competing Psychological Theories
  4   What Makes a Horror Movie Good?

C **Scan paragraph D.** Underline the three components of horror movies.

OUR ATTRACTION TO
FRIGHT

A 🎧 **9.7** Do you enjoy watching horror movies? Many people do, and scientists are interested in finding out why.

B Millions of years of human evolution have made us afraid of certain things. For example, we are afraid of the dark for good reason—sometimes wild animals or other dangers hide in the dark. In a way, fear has helped humans avoid danger and has helped us survive.

C _____ Scientists have **identified** an area of the brain that is linked to fear: the amygdala. This area of the brain produces stronger **responses** when people view pictures of animals—compared to pictures of people, places, or objects. Perhaps this is why so many scary movies have animal-like monsters. However, brain research also shows that horror movies don't actually create fear responses in the amygdala. This makes researchers **curious** to know the kinds of emotions people are really feeling when they watch a horror movie.

D _____ It's important to understand what creates horror in movies. Psychologist Glenn D. Walters has identified three **factors**. One is tension, created through mystery, fear, shock, and **mood**. The second is relevance: There are basic fears we all share, such as fear of the unknown. The third factor is unrealism. In one study, students were shown horrible scenes from documentaries. Most students couldn't watch them. But these same students paid money to see even worse scenes in horror movies. Why? They knew the movie was not real.

E _____ The attraction to fear is interesting on a psychological level. Many theories have tried to explain its **appeal**. One theory suggests that young people like horror movies because adults tend to frown upon them or think that horror movies are not suitable for young viewers. For adults, the appeal may be a sort of dark curiosity, similar to what happens when we stop to look at a car accident. Another theory claims that people enjoy watching horror movies because of the feeling of confidence they experience afterward.

F Although many theories have been suggested, we still don't fully understand our fascination with horror movies. But whatever reasons people have for watching them, one thing is clear—horror movies are not going anywhere.

COMPREHENSION

A Answer the questions about *Our Attraction to Fright*.

IDIOM

Someone who is very scared is "scared _____ ."
a stone
b scream
c stiff

1 **PURPOSE** The main purpose of paragraph B is to _____ .

   a give an introduction to human evolution

   b list the reasons why some people are scared of the dark

   c explain why we fear some things

2 **INFERENCE** Horror movies often make use of music to add to the _____ .

   a tension   b relevance   c unrealism

3 **DETAIL** It's easier for people to watch scary scenes in movies than in documentaries because they know that the scenes in movies _____ .

   a aren't real   b aren't important   c aren't as exciting

4 **VOCABULARY** In paragraph E, *frown upon* means _____ .

   a to be unafraid of

   b to show disapproval of

   c to refuse to see

5 **COHESION** The following sentence would best be placed at the end of which paragraph?

   They feel better about themselves because they made it through the horror safely.

   a paragraph C   b paragraph D   c paragraph E

B Read the statements. Circle T for true, F for false, or NG for not given.

1 There are evolutionary reasons for why we fear certain things.   **T   F   NG**

2 The amygdala responds more strongly to pictures of places   **T   F   NG**
   than of objects.

3 Scary movies activate fear responses in the amygdala.   **T   F   NG**

4 One way to build tension in a movie is through the use of   **T   F   NG**
   mystery.

5 People in their 20s watch more horror movies than anyone else.   **T   F   NG**

C CRITICAL THINKING Justifying an Opinion Talk with a partner. Do you think watching horror movies is harmful in any way? Give reasons for your opinion.

VOCABULARY

A **Find the words below in the article.** Then complete the sentences using the words in the box.

| appeal | curious | factors | identify | mood | response |

1 Your _____ to an action or event is your reaction to it.

2 The _____ of something is what makes it attractive or interesting to others.

3 The _____ of a story is the general feeling that you get from it.

4 When you _____ something, you discover its existence and are able to name it.

5 _____ are the parts or elements that contribute to a particular result.

6 If you are _____ about something, you are interested in it and want to know more about it.

B **Read the information below.** Then write true sentences using the words in **bold** (1–4).

> One way to help remember new vocabulary is to write true sentences using each word. This gives you a personal connection to the word, helping you to remember it more easily.
>
> **horror:** *Horror movies scare most people, but not me.*

1 **afraid:** _____

2 **tension:** _____

3 **horrible:** _____

4 **fascination:** _____

WRITING

A **Read the movie review.**

B **Choose a movie you watched recently.** Make notes about it.

C **Write a movie review using your notes.** Describe the movie and share what you liked or didn't like about it.

MovieReviewForum.com

MOVIE REVIEW

A fun family movie ★★★★☆

I watched *Aladdin* recently. The movie is a live-action remake of Disney's 1992 animated film of the same name. I really liked the music and the characters, especially the Genie, who was played by Will Smith. I would recommend this movie to everyone because …

FREE SOLO

Before You Watch

Work with a partner. You are going to watch the trailer for the documentary *Free Solo*. What makes a good movie trailer? What should a trailer include? Note your ideas.

While You Watch

A ▶ 9.2 **Watch the video.** Based on the trailer, what would you expect to see in the documentary?

   a Alex Honnold's attempt to climb El Capitan in record time

   b Alex Honnold's quest to climb El Capitan without ropes or equipment

   c how a team of climbers rescued Alex Honnold after he fell from El Capitan

B ▶ 9.2 **Watch again.** Circle the correct answers.

   1 Alex says that having a girlfriend makes his life **better in every way** / **harder in some ways**.

   2 Alex's girlfriend **is** / **isn't** interviewed in the documentary.

   3 The director Jimmy Chin has mixed feelings about shooting the film because **he almost died once while climbing El Capitan** / **he's afraid that Alex will fall and die**.

C **Look at these expressions from the video.** Choose the correct meanings of the words in **bold**.

   1 "People who really know exactly what he's doing are **freaked out**."

     a extremely happy   **b** very anxious

   2 "I'm starting to **get kind of psyched**."

     a feel a little scared   **b** become very excited

   3 "Hey, Jimmy, **do you copy**? Just started climbing."

     a do you hear me   **b** are you doing the same thing as me

After You Watch

Talk with a partner. Look back at your notes from **Before You Watch**. Assess the trailer for *Free Solo*. Does it meet your criteria for a good movie trailer? Did it make you want to watch *Free Solo*?

Alex Honnold (in red) training for his free solo climb up El Capitan, or El Cap, in Yosemite National Park

A **Complete the sentences.** Circle the correct answers.

1 The acting was **overrated** / **superb**. It was some of the best I've ever seen.

2 The costumes were **spectacular** / **uninteresting**. Everyone looked amazing.

3 I found the movie's plot quite **exciting** / **dull**. I fell asleep in the theater!

4 The characters are so **predictable** / **unrealistic**. No one behaves or talks that way.

B **Complete the questions.** Write appropriate tag forms.

1 Your sister has acted in a movie, _____?

2 They're not planning to see the movie tonight, _____?

3 He went to the wrong movie theater, _____?

4 You can't see that movie without a parent, _____?

5 You haven't bought tickets for the movie yet, _____?

C **Complete the sentences.** Use the words in the box.

afraid	fascination	horrible	tension

1 The sight was so _____ that I had to turn away.

2 Why do some people have such a(n) _____ with snakes? I find them terrifying.

3 I wasn't _____ while watching the movie, but the music did create some _____ .

SELF CHECK   Now I can …

☐ talk about what makes movies successful or unsuccessful

☐ ask for confirmation or information

☐ discuss why people enjoy feeling scared

I WISH
I COULD BE AN
OLYMPIC
ATHLETE!

A ski jumper in mid-air

PREVIEW

A 🎧 **10.1 Listen.** Four students are discussing their wishes. Number the wishes (1–4).

_____ cure diseases

_____ be an athlete

_____ travel back in time

_____ be a famous architect

B 🎧 **10.1 Listen again.** What would the students do if their wishes came true? Write two words for each blank.

1 John would meet Albert Einstein and

_____ .

2 Gabriela would set a(n)

_____ .

3 Luke would design

_____ .

4 Sara would find a cure

_____ .

C **Talk with a partner.** Look at the wishes in **A**. Which wish would you choose? Why?

> I wish I could travel back in time. That way, I could find the answers to ancient mysteries!

> When would you go back to?

PEOPLE AND PLACES

UNIT GOALS

- talk about your wishes and hopes

- learn language for talking about wishes and imaginary situations

- learn about teenagers who are making a difference in the world

LANGUAGE FOCUS

A 🎧 **10.2 Listen and read.** What superpower would Stig like to have? Then repeat the conversation and replace the words in **bold**.

> **REAL ENGLISH** You mean …?

Stig: Do you ever wish you had a superpower?

Ming: You mean like being able to **fly**?
(**see through walls / travel back in time**)

Stig: Yeah. What do you wish you could do?

Ming: I wish I could breathe underwater.

Stig: That would be **cool**! (**awesome / amazing**)

Ming: What superpower would you **want to have**?
(**like to have / wish for**)

Stig: I'd want to control people's minds.

Ming: Why's that?

Stig: If I could do that, I could make **all my teachers give me A's**!
(**other people do all my chores /
my friends buy me food every day**)

B 🎧 **10.3 Look at the chart.** Then circle the correct answers below.

TALKING ABOUT WISHES AND IMAGINARY SITUATIONS (USING *WISH*, *WOULD* + VERB)	
I **wish** I	**were** famous. / **didn't have** so much homework. / **could play** an instrument.
If you **were** rich, **would** you **use** the money to travel?	Yes, I **would**. I'**d use** it to go to Antarctica. No, I **wouldn't**. I'**d donate** the money to charity.
If you **could have** any superpower, what **would** it **be**?	I'**d like** to be able to fly.
Where **would** you **go if** you **could go** anywhere in the world?	**If** I **could go** anywhere in the world, I'**d go** to Australia and New Zealand.

1 The examples in the chart refer to imaginary situations in the **past** / **present or future**.

2 We talk about wishes using subject + *wish* + subject + the **past** / **present** tense.

3 When talking about unlikely or imaginary situations, we use the **past** / **present** tense in the *if*-clause and **will** / **would** + base verb in the main clause.

C **Complete the sentences.** Use the correct form of the phrases in the box.

> be older   be more hours in a day   ~~can go back in time~~
> can sing well   be fewer words in English

1 I wish I _____ *could go back in time* _____ . It would be interesting to meet Abraham Lincoln.

2 I'm too young to drive. I wish I _____ .

3 I never have enough time to see my friends. I wish there _____ .

4 I wish I _____ . It would be fun to enter a talent competition.

5 I wish there _____ . There are too many to remember!

D 🎧 **10.4** **Complete the conversations.** Write the correct form of the words in parentheses. Use contractions where possible. Then listen and check your answers.

1 **Kay:** What would you do if you [1] _____ (**be**) rich?

   Hugh: I [2] _____ (**buy**) a nice house for my parents.

2 **Ahmed:** If you [3] _____ (**can have**) any superpower, what superpower
[4] _____ you _____ (**want**)?

   Sandy: I think I'd want to be able to predict the future.

3 **Erin:** If you [5] _____ (**can live**) forever, would you be happy?

   Bruno: No way. I [6] _____ (**not want**) that.

4 **Trevor:** If you [7] _____ (**not have to**) go to school, how different would your life be?

   Haruko: It [8] _____ (**not be**) different at all. I'd still want to go to school.

E **Work in groups.** Imagine you have been granted three wishes. What would you wish for? Share your wishes with your group members.

I wish I could talk to animals.

Why?

I'd like to know what they think of us.

WHAT *SUPERPOWER* DO YOU WISH *YOU HAD?*

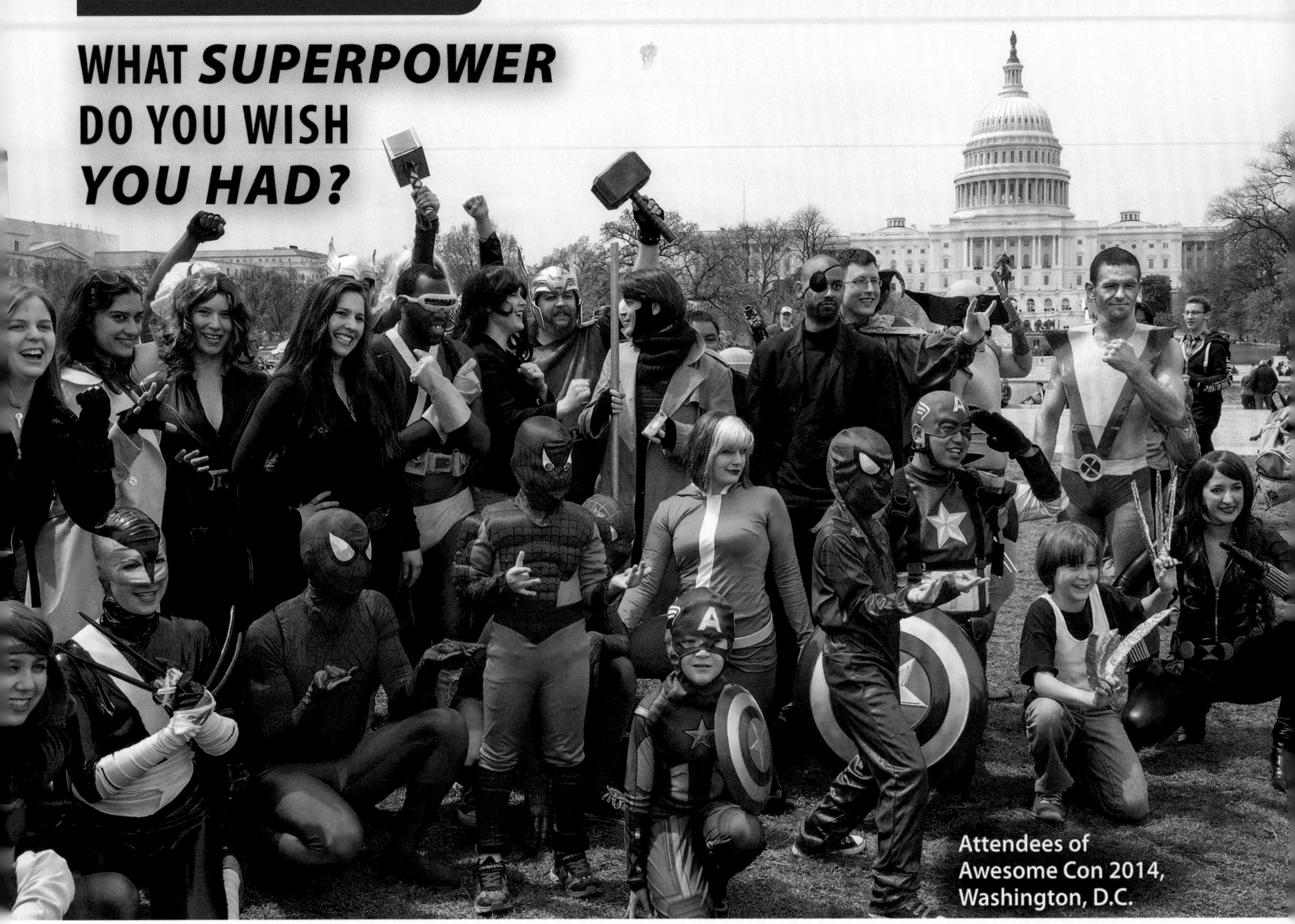

Attendees of Awesome Con 2014, Washington, D.C.

A ▶ 10.1 **Predict.** You are going to watch 10 National Geographic Explorers talk about superpowers they wish they had. What do you think is the most common wish? Circle **a**, **b**, or **c**. Then watch the video and check your prediction.

a to be able to read people's minds

b to be able to fly

c to be invisible

DO YOU KNOW?

Some people say you should make a wish if a _____ lands on your hand.

a moth
b blackbird
c ladybug

B ▶ 10.1 **Watch again.** Match each Explorer with the superpower they wish they had.

1 Andrés Ruzo ○ ○ the ability to magically make people understand

2 Neil deGrasse Tyson ○ ○ invisibility

3 Ricky Qi ○ ○ the power to read other people's minds

4 Albert Lin ○ ○ the power to turn anything into any kind of food

C **Complete these sentences describing real superhuman abilities.** Circle the correct answers. Which ability do you think is the most incredible?

1 In 2006, American Dean Karnazes ran **5 / 50** marathons in 50 days, in all 50 U.S. states.

2 Anne Jones, a retired teacher from England, can read up to **470 / 4,700** words in one minute. The average adult can read 220–300 words per minute.

3 Known as the "human computer," Shakuntala Devi of India could solve 7,686,369,774,870 × 2,465,099,745,779 in 28 **seconds / minutes**—in her head.

D **CRITICAL THINKING Ranking** **Of the superpowers below, which appeals to you the most?** Rank them from **1** (most appealing) to **3** (least appealing). Then share your ranking and reasons with a partner.

_____ being able to fly   _____ being able to teleport   _____ being invisible

PROJECT Talk to three family members. Ask them what superpower they wish they had. Share their answers with a partner.

PRONUNCIATION contractions: *'ll* and *'d*

🎧 **10.5** **Listen.** Circle the words you hear. Then listen again and repeat the sentences.

1 **I'll / I'd** go to the White House.

2 **He'll / He'd** visit Brazil.

3 **She'll / She'd** be a famous athlete.

4 **I'll / I'd** buy a new car.

COMMUNICATION

Play a game. Work with a partner. Read the questions below. Guess what your partner's answers will be. Then check your guesses and ask follow-up questions.

Questions	My guesses	My partner's answers
Which would you choose to spend one day as—a cat or a bird?		
If you could be very rich or very good-looking, which would you choose?		
If you had to give up pizza or burgers, which would you never eat again?		
If you had to lose your hearing or your sense of taste, which would it be?		

Which would you choose to spend one day as—a cat or a bird?

I'd be a cat.

Oh, I didn't guess that correctly. Why would you want to be a cat?

READING

A Read the title. What does it mean to "make a difference"?

a become famous by accident

b do the opposite of what others say or do

c have a positive impact on a person or situation

B Scan the article. Where are the teenagers from? Underline the places.

C Talk with a partner. Do you know of other young people who have made a difference in the world? What did they do?

Kelvin Doe

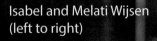
Isabel and Melati Wijsen (left to right)

MAKING A
DIFFERENCE

🎧 10.6 The Inventor

Kelvin Doe was born during Sierra Leone's civil war. He was six when the war ended. Today, he **represents** how this West African country is moving forward. A short film about him has already been viewed millions of times on YouTube.

Kelvin is a self-taught engineer. At age 11, he began digging through trash to find electronic parts to create things. Since then, he has built a battery, a generator to provide electricity, and a radio station from recycled materials.

At age 15, Kelvin won a competition that took him to the United States. There, he spoke to students about his **inventions**. He also appeared on television, and was a speaker at TEDxTeen. He has helped **inspire** and educate people through these **events**.

The Environmentalists

Melati Wijsen, 18, and her sister Isabel, 16, are fighting plastic pollution in their home of Bali, in Indonesia. In 2013, they started a campaign called Bye Bye Plastic Bags, after being inspired by a school lesson on significant people. They went home that day and asked themselves, "What can we do now, as children living in Bali, to make a difference?" The answer was right in front of them, on the plastic-covered beach.

The sisters organized beach cleanups, collected signatures calling for a ban on single-use plastic bags, and used social media to **pressure** the local government. They even gave a TED Talk. Their efforts paid off. In 2019, the governor of Bali announced a ban on single-use plastics. The sisters are thrilled, but want to do more to reduce plastic pollution around the world.

The Journalist

Like many teenagers in Rio de Janeiro, Rene Silva is interested in computer games, soccer, and music. But he also has another interest—he wants people to understand what the poor neighborhoods, or *favelas*, are really like. Many people see Rio's favelas as dangerous places. Rene has used social media to show a more positive side.

When Rene was 11, he set up a neighborhood newspaper for his favela. He worked hard writing reports for the paper. At 17, he became famous for tweeting about a police raid there. On his blog, he corrected mistakes made by TV reporters. Soon, his followers increased from a few hundred to tens of thousands.

At age 19, Rene wrote his first book about the favelas. If he could have one wish, it would be to educate others about the people living there. "Today," Rene says, "there is more recognition of the people who are trying to do good and change the **reality** of the place where they live."

COMPREHENSION

A **Answer the questions about *Making a Difference*.**

1 (DETAIL) According to the article, what is true about Kelvin Doe?

   a He fought in Sierra Leone's civil war.

   b He studied engineering in the United States.

   c He taught himself how to make a generator.

2 (CAUSE-EFFECT) What gave Melati and Isabel Wijsen the idea to start Bye Bye Plastic Bags?

   a learning about plastic pollution at school

   b realizing how much plastic they use

   c seeing plastic trash on a beach

3 (VOCABULARY) In line 22, *paid off* means _____.

   a received a big donation   **b** resulted in success   **c** became well known

4 (DETAIL) Rene Silva is trying to _____ in Rio's favelas.

   a improve children's access to education

   b educate people about life

   c create more job opportunities

5 (SEQUENCE) Which activity happened last?

   a Rene wrote a book about the favelas.

   b Rene set up a newspaper in his neighborhood.

   c Rene became famous for tweeting about a police raid.

B **Look at the descriptions (a–g) below.**
Write them in the Venn diagram.

   a wrote a book
   b won a competition
   c used social media
   d started a newspaper
   e was/were inspired by a school lesson
   f is/are involved in recycling or reducing pollution
   g is/are using their influence to educate people

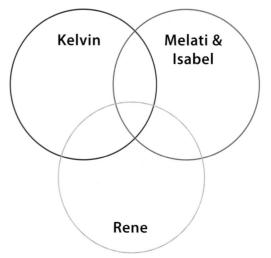

C (CRITICAL THINKING Applying) **Talk with a partner.** In what way(s) could you make a difference in your community?

VOCABULARY

A **Find the bold words below in the article.** Then circle the correct answers.

1 If you **represent** a country, you *are a symbol of it / leave it for another place*.

2 Examples of **inventions** include *TVs and computers / happiness and excitement*.

3 If you **inspire** people to do something, they *no longer want / have a strong desire* to do it.

4 An example of an **event** is a high school *dance / teacher*.

5 If you **pressure** someone, you *take a photo of them / try to persuade them to do something*.

6 The **reality** of a situation is how *it actually is / you wish it was*.

IDIOM

If something is "beyond your wildest dreams," it's _____ you imagined.
a worse than
b exactly as
c better than

B **Read the information below.** Then complete the sentences (1–4) with expressions from the box. Two expressions are extra.

> There are many expressions containing the word *wish*:
>
> make a wish   wish list   against (someone's) wishes
>
> grant a wish   dying wish   wish (someone) good luck

1 My grandmother's _____ was to see the ocean one last time.

2 Be sure to _____ before you blow out the candles on your birthday cake.

3 My cousin called to _____ me _____ in my new job.

4 She was angry because her brother posted a photo of her on Facebook _____ her _____.

WRITING

A **Read the blog post.**

B **Think about three changes you would like to see in the world.** Note your ideas.

C **Write a blog post using your notes.** What three changes would you wish for? What would you do to make these changes happen?

HOME   ABOUT   **BLOG**   FAQ   CONTACT

I think education is very important, so one of my wishes is to see every child being able to go to school. If I were in the government, I would make it possible for poor children to receive an education by ...

ROBOBEES

Before You Watch

Look at the photo below. What do you think Robert Wood's robots are like?
Check (✓) the features.

- ☐ small
- ☐ cheaper to make
- ☐ can lift heavy things
- ☐ soft
- ☐ can fly
- ☐ built from recycled materials

While You Watch

A ▶ 10.2 **Watch the video.** Check your answers to the **Before You Watch** question.

B ▶ 10.2 **Watch again.** Circle the correct answers.

1 Robert hopes his robots will be useful in **exploring space and deep oceans** /
   monitoring people's health.

2 Robert's team gets ideas from **nature** / **machines**.

3 Robert believes that in the next **5** / **20** years, his robots will be able to help people
   do dangerous tasks.

4 Robert's team wants to build robots that **work in groups like** /
   are as independent as bees.

C **Discuss with a partner.** How effective do you think Robert's robot insects will be at these
tasks? Would success require a single RoboBee or a group of RoboBees?

detecting gas leaks	surveying disaster zones	pollinating crops
delivering supplies	spying on people	tracking marine life

After You Watch

Talk with a partner. If you could
build a robot, what kind of robot
would you want to build?

A robot created
by Robert Wood
and his team

A Complete the sentences. Use the phrases in the box (**a–d**).

> **a** cure diseases   **c** play a musical instrument
> **b** meet someone famous   **d** travel back in time

1 I wish I could _____ . It would be cool to see real dinosaurs.

2 I wish I could _____ . Then people would live much longer.

3 I wish I could _____ . It would be fun to perform with a band.

4 I wish I could _____ . If I had a choice, I'd meet Barack Obama.

B Complete the sentences. Write the correct form of the words in parentheses. Use contractions where possible.

1 If I _____ (**can cure**) only one disease,

   I _____ (**cure**) diabetes.

2 If you _____ (**be**) rich, what _____ you

   _____ (**buy**) first?

3 Bryan _____ (**wish**) he _____ (**not have**)
so much homework every week.

4 Sebastian _____ (**not attend**) school if he
_____ (**not have to**).

C Complete the sentences. Use the words in the box. Two words are extra.

> against   good   grant   list   luck   make

1 Visiting Japan is at the top of my wish _____ .

2 Hae-Soon went to the party _____ her mother's wishes.

3 I'd like to wish everyone _____ _____ for the
exam tomorrow.

SELF CHECK   Now I can …

☐ talk about my wishes and hopes

☐ use language for talking about wishes and imaginary
situations

☐ talk about teenagers who are making a difference in
the world

WHAT
WOULD
YOU
DO?

What would you do if you saw someone being pickpocketed?

PREVIEW

A 🎧 **11.1** **Listen.** What situations are these people facing? Circle the correct answers.

1 Susan saw someone **stealing / cheating**.

   Friend's advice:

   _____

2 Matt's neighbors refused to **turn down their music / clear their trash**.

   Friend's advice:

   _____

3 May **lost / damaged** something in a store.

   Friend's advice:

   _____

4 Robert found a **handbag / wallet** on the sidewalk.

   Friend's advice:

   _____

B 🎧 **11.2** **Listen.** What is their friend's advice? Fill in the blanks in **A**.

C **Talk with a partner.** Do you agree with the friend's advice? What would you do in each situation in **A**?

> I think Susan's friend gave good advice. I'd probably do the same thing.

> I disagree. I think …

HISTORY AND CULTURE

UNIT GOALS

- discuss ethical dilemmas

- review previously learned language

- learn about different aspects of lying

LANGUAGE FOCUS

A 🎧 **11.3** **Listen and read.** What problem does Nadine have? Then repeat the conversation and replace the words in **bold**.

> **REAL ENGLISH** What a relief!

Ming: **Is everything OK**, Nadine? (**Is something the matter / Are you OK**)

Nadine: I've been thinking all day about this problem I have.

Ming: **What kind of problem**? Maybe I can help. (**What's bothering you / What is it**)

Nadine: What would you do if you lost something that you borrowed from a friend?

Ming: I'd apologize and tell the friend the truth.

Nadine: And if you were that friend, **you'd be angry, wouldn't you**? (**would you be angry / don't you think you'd be angry**)

Ming: Not at all! Everyone makes mistakes.

Nadine: What a relief! So … remember that **video game** I borrowed? (**book / scarf**)

B 🎧 **11.4** **Look at the chart.** Then circle the correct answers below.

LANGUAGE REVIEW	
Present perfect progressive and passive form	**Describing probability**
She**'s been waiting** here for an hour.	You **must** be very relieved.
My neighbor **was taken** to the hospital.	This bag **could/might** belong to Ben.
Giving advice and talking about imaginary situations	That **can't** be her car. Hers is black.
	He **could/might** have taken the wallet.
You **should apologize** for saying that.	I **must** have left my homework at home.
If I **saw** a crime, I**'d call** the police.	She **couldn't** have left the book there.

1 We use **should** / **will** + base verb to give advice.

2 In passive sentences, the person who does the action **is** / **isn't** always important.

3 We use *must* when we are **very** / **not very** sure about something.

C 🎧 **11.5** **Complete the conversations.** Circle the correct answers. Then listen and check.

1 Amy: If you had an extra $1,000, what [1] **would** / **must** you do with it?

Hector: That's a lot of money. [2] **I'd** / **I'll** buy a new computer. [3] **I was using** / **I've been using** this one for five years.

2 Seo-jun: I heard that the answers to today's test [4] **were being stolen** / **were stolen**. They [5] **took** / **were taken** off Mr. Lee's desk when he left to make a call.

Kelly: No way! Does he know who [6] **did** / **was done** it?

3 Peter: Do you know whose backpack this is?

Isobel: It [7] **would** / **might** be Jennifer's. She has a blue bag.

Peter: No, it [8] **can't be** / **might not have been** hers. Look—the initials "T. R." are on it.

D **Complete the sentences.** Use your own ideas.

1 Feng was up all night studying. She must _____ now.

2 I don't see Richard anywhere. He must have _____ .

3 If you need career advice, I think you should _____ .

4 Allie has been _____ for over a year.

E **Work in groups.** Talk about what you would do in each situation below.

- You are given the ability to communicate with one animal species.
- You accidentally break the handle off a mug in a store.
- You see your favorite celebrity on the street.
- You are mistakenly given an A+ by your teacher.
- You can go back in time and change one historical event.
- You are allowed to change one law in your country.

What would you do if you were given the ability to communicate with one animal species?

I'd communicate with humpback whales. I'd want to know …

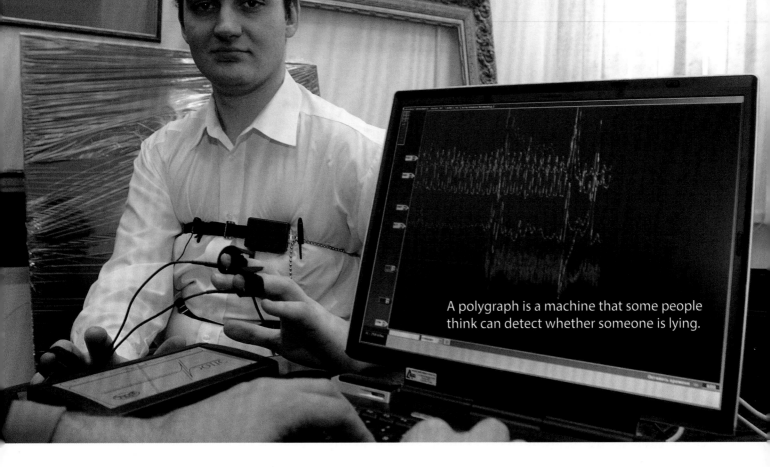

WHY WE LIE

A polygraph is a machine that some people think can detect whether someone is lying.

A ▶ 11.1 **Guess the answers to these questions.** Then watch **Part 1** of the video and check your guesses.

1 How many times a day do adults lie on average?

   a 1–2   **b** 5–6   **c** 10–12

2 Which age group lies the most?

   a people aged 6–8   **b** people aged 13–17   **c** people aged 25–35

3 Which age group lies the least?

   a people aged 6–8   **b** people aged 13–17   **c** people aged 25–35

B ▶ 11.2 **Watch Part 2 of the video.** Complete the summary below using words from the video.

Most lies are told so that people can [1] _____ or promote themselves. Fewer lies are told for the sake of other people. For example, we lie to cover up our [2] _____, to avoid other people, to gain economic and personal [3] _____, or even to make people laugh.

C **Read these examples of lies.** Write the reason for each lie: **a** = to protect yourself, **b** = to promote yourself, or **c** = to help or hurt someone else.

1 You don't like Seth, so you told him you have to work on Friday so that you won't have to see him. _____

2 You were mad at your coworker, so you told everyone that she was stealing money. _____

3 You told someone that you can speak five languages, which isn't true. _____

4 Your little brother broke a vase in a store, but you said that you did it. _____

5 You spilled juice on the kitchen floor but told your parents that the cat knocked it off the table. _____

D CRITICAL THINKING Reflecting **Talk with a partner.** In the video, Erika Bergman says people lie "because it's easy." Do you agree? Is it ever OK to lie? If so, under what circumstances?

PROJECT Think about the last lie you told. When was it? Why did you lie? If you faced the same situation, would you lie again?

PRONUNCIATION final *t* or *d* with initial *y*

A 🎧 11.6 **Listen and repeat.**

1 I want you to be honest.   2 What would you do?

B 🎧 11.7 **Listen.** Write the words you hear. Then listen again and repeat the sentences.

1 How _____ get here?

2 I don't _____ to be angry.

3 _____ like to play a game?

4 Why won't the teacher _____ leave early?

DO YOU KNOW?

When making moral decisions, people tend to use areas of the brain related to

_____ .
a emotion
b logic

COMMUNICATION

Debate an issue. Your school wants to ban cell phones in class. Work in groups of four. Two students are Team A, and two students are Team B. **Team A:** Turn to page 150. **Team B:** Turn to page 152.

We don't support the ban because we think cell phone use promotes critical thinking. For example, …

READING

A Look at the title. What do you think thought experiments are?

B Scan the first paragraph. Who designs thought experiments?

C Read the article. As you read, think about what you would do in each situation. Share your ideas with a partner.

THOUGHT EXPERIMENTS

🎧 **11.8** Like scientists, philosophers use **experiments** to test their ideas. But unlike scientists, they don't need labs or expensive equipment. Instead, they use moral dilemmas to better understand the human mind. Moral dilemmas are situations where a difficult decision has to be made.
5 There are no right or wrong answers to the questions raised by the following thought experiments.

The Runaway Train

You are walking along some train tracks. You look ahead and see five people—they've been tied up and left on the tracks. They're unable to
10 move and are shouting for help. An out-of-control train is speeding toward them. It's going to hit and kill them if you do nothing.

You see that the train tracks **split**. Next to you is a lever. All you need to do is pull the lever to make the train go onto the other track. However, a person is crossing that other track. If you pull the lever, the train will
15 kill the lone person, but you'll save the five people who are tied up.

The Prisoner's Dilemma

You and a friend **robbed** a bank, and both of you have been arrested. You are brought to the police station and placed in two different rooms.

A police officer comes in and questions you. You can either remain silent
20 or **blame** your friend for the **crime**. If you blame your friend and your friend remains silent, you can go free and your friend will go to prison for five years. If you remain silent but your friend blames you, your friend will go free and you'll go to prison for five years. If you both blame each other, you'll both go to prison for three years. If you both remain silent, you'll
25 both go to prison for only one year.

The Famous Pianist

You wake up and find yourself in a hospital bed, covered with tubes. These tubes **connect** you to a famous pianist. The pianist is very sick, and only your blood type can save him. He'll die if you remove the tubes now.
30 On the other hand, if you choose to remain connected for the next three months, he'll definitely get better. Although you have to stay in bed for three months, there'll be no danger to your health.

What would you do in each of these situations? Philosophers are very interested in studying the different responses people give. They want to
35 find out how people think or react in various situations.

COMPREHENSION

A Answer the questions about *Thought Experiments*.

1 MAIN IDEA What is true about thought experiments?

   a They were first created by scientists.

   b They have a single correct answer.

   c They are used to test the human mind.

2 DETAIL In "The Runaway Train," if you want to let things happen naturally, you'd _____ .

   a get help   **b** pull the lever   **c** do nothing

3 VOCABULARY Which of the following has a different meaning from the word *lone* in line 15?

   a single   **b** lonely   **c** solitary

4 DETAIL In "The Prisoner's Dilemma," is it possible for you to avoid prison time?

   a Yes, if you blame your friend.

   b Yes, if you remain silent.

   c No, it isn't possible.

5 INFERENCE Which of the following is NOT true in the case of "The Famous Pianist"?

   a You have a very rare blood type.

   b To help the pianist, you'll have to break the law.

   c It involves a life-or-death decision.

> **IDIOM**
>
> If someone is "between a rock and a hard place," the person is in a situation with _____ choices.
> **a** unpleasant
> **b** confusing
> **c** too many

B Match each thought experiment with the question it raises.

1 "The Runaway Train" ◯   ◯ Should you make personal sacrifices to help someone live?

2 "The Prisoner's Dilemma" ◯   ◯ Is there a difference between killing someone and allowing them to be killed?

3 "The Famous Pianist" ◯   ◯ Do you trust someone enough?

C CRITICAL THINKING Evaluating Talk with a partner. Would your responses to the thought experiments depend on other factors not mentioned in the article? What kinds of factors would change your decisions?

VOCABULARY

A **Find the words below in the article.** Then complete the sentences using the correct form of the words in the box.

blame	connect	crime	experiment	rob	split

1 A hallway _____ the bedroom to the living room.

2 The two men _____ a department store and stole thousands of dollars.

3 The _____ is designed to test why some people lie more than others.

4 Shoplifting is a serious _____ .

5 I don't _____ anyone for the accident but myself.

6 Turn right where the road _____ , then continue walking.

B **Read the information below.** Complete the sentences (1–4) with the words in the box. Then decide if each sentence is in the present or past tense, and circle your answer.

> Some verbs, such as *split* and *cut*, have the same form in the simple present tense and in the simple past tense. You can usually determine which tense is being used from the context.

cut	hurt	quit	split

1 She _____ her job after only two weeks.   **present**   **past**

2 My knees _____ , so I think I should see a doctor.   **present**   **past**

3 The teacher _____ the class into three groups.   **present**   **past**

4 This knife doesn't _____ very well.   **present**   **past**

WRITING

A **Read the paragraph.**

B **Do you think this project is a good idea?** Why or why not? Make a list of pros and cons, and choose a side.

C **Write a persuasive essay.** Introduce the topic and present your point of view. Give reasons for your argument.

A developer has proposed turning a large area of forested land on the edge of town into a new mall. Some local residents are for the project, but some aren't. I support this project because I think it will bring many benefits to the town. Firstly, ...

TEST OF CHARACTER

Before You Watch

Talk with a partner. In an experiment, a lone person sees a thief trying to steal a woman's handbag. The experiment was conducted 10 times. How many people do you think tried to help the woman?

While You Watch

A   ▶ 11.3   **Watch Part 1 of the video.** Match the people below with their reactions.

1	2	3
○	○	○
○	○	○
helps the woman	watches but does nothing	runs away

B   ▶ 11.4   **Watch Part 2 of the video.** Complete the summary of the experiment.

The experiment took place in a restaurant with hidden ¹ _____ . An actor walked past customers and fell to the ground. The lone diner took ² _____ seconds to help the man. The group of diners took ³ _____ seconds. This is an example of the "bystander effect." When people are in a group, they wait for ⁴ _____ to take control.

C   **Read the information below.** What kind of impact do you think social media has on the bystander effect? Do you know of any other situations like this? Discuss in groups.

> In 2013, a fire broke out on a residential street in Pincourt, Canada. Observers took videos of the house burning to the ground and uploaded them to social media—but nobody called the fire department.

After You Watch

Talk with a partner. Describe an actual situation where you needed to help someone. What did you do? Have you ever been affected by the bystander effect?

REVIEW

A Complete the sentences. Use the words in the box.

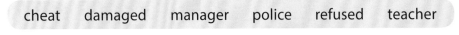

> cheat   damaged   manager   police   refused   teacher

1 I saw a classmate _____ on the exam today. Should I tell the _____ ?

2 I was in a café last night, and two customers got into a fight. They _____ some of the furniture but _____ to apologize to the owner.

3 Someone broke into my apartment while I was out. I called the _____ of my apartment block as soon as I got home. She then called the _____ .

B Complete the sentences. Circle the correct answers.

1 I'm so happy that the baby panda **rescued** / **was rescued**.

2 I'd help if I saw someone **fall** / **fell** to the floor.

3 You got 100 percent on the exam? You **must be** / **might have been** thrilled!

4 You're the one who broke the glass. You **would** / **should** apologize.

5 Mariko **to lie** / **has been lying** about her age for a long time.

C Complete the sentences. Use the words in parentheses. In each set, one word is extra.

1 Did it _____ when you _____ your finger? (*cut*, *hurt*, *quit*)

2 Tony _____ the race after he fell and _____ himself. (*hurt*, *quit*, *split*)

SELF CHECK   Now I can …

☐ discuss ethical dilemmas

☐ use previously learned language

☐ talk about why people lie

WHOLE GRAINS
ARE GOOD
FOR YOU

There are several health benefits to eating rye bread.

PREVIEW

A 🎧 **12.1 Listen.** Match the types of food with their benefits.

1 vegetables and fruits ○ ○ provide you with energy

2 whole grains ○ ○ great source of protein

3 meat and poultry ○ ○ good for your heart

4 foods containing healthy fats ○ ○ full of vitamins and minerals

B 🎧 **12.1 Listen again.** Circle **T** for true or **F** for false.

1 The body breaks down whole grains quickly. **T   F**

2 You should increase the amount of red meat in your diet. **T   F**

3 Eating too much salt can lead to high blood pressure. **T   F**

4 Fresh juice is the best drink for your body. **T   F**

C Talk with a partner. What are some healthy foods that you like?

> I like eating carrots. They're sweet and good for you.

> I love yogurt. I heard that eating it after exercising helps your body recover faster.

SCIENCE AND TECHNOLOGY

UNIT GOALS

• talk about health and nutrition

• review previously learned language

• learn about the human brain

LANGUAGE FOCUS

A 🎧 **12.2 Listen and read.** Why doesn't Maya give advice to Nadine? Then repeat the conversation and replace the words in **bold**.

REAL ENGLISH   Any ideas?

Nadine: I have **too many things to do**. I'm so stressed out! (**such a busy schedule / so many things I need to do**)

Stig: You should try to relax.

Nadine: That's easier said than done. Any ideas?

Stig: Well, **exercising** is a great way to relax. (**meditating / reading**)

Nadine: Yeah, I know. It's just hard to find the time sometimes.

Ming: And you should think about reducing the amount of **coffee** you drink. (**soda / tea**)

Nadine: I do drink a lot of **coffee**, don't I? (**soda / tea**)

Stig: What's your advice, Maya?

Nadine: If Maya were awake, she'd tell me **to take a nap**! (**to get plenty of sleep / that sleeping is the best way to relax**)

B 🎧 **12.3 Look at the chart.** Then circle the correct answers below.

LANGUAGE REVIEW	
Gerunds	**Tag questions**
Exercising is a great way to relax.	Nuts **are** good for you, **aren't they**?
Describing and comparing things	**Non-defining relative clauses**
This banana is (**not**) **as ripe as** that one. I'm not going out today. I'm **too tired**. This coffee is (**not**) **sweet enough**.	My aunt, **who studied medicine**, always gives good health advice. Greek yogurt, **which has a lot of protein**, is good for you.

1 We use **adjective + enough** / **as + adjective + as** to say that two things are equal.

2 Tag questions can be used to **check / add** information.

3 If we remove a non-defining relative clause from a sentence, the sentence **still makes** / **makes no** sense.

C 🎧 12.4 **Complete the paragraph.** Circle the correct answers. Then listen and check.

Having a good night's sleep feels great, [1] **does / doesn't** it? [2] **Get / Getting** the right amount of sleep is important for teens, [3] **who / which** need energy to study or play sports. But during the teenage years, there is a reset of the body's internal "clock." This reset tells a person to fall asleep later and wake up later. Many teens don't get [4] **sleep enough / enough sleep** because they go to sleep late but wake up early for school. School life is busy, and getting through a full day without enough rest isn't as [5] **easy / easier** as you might think. So, if you're feeling [6] **too tired / tired enough** to give your best during the day, you're probably not getting the eight to nine hours of sleep experts say you need.

D **Match the phrases to form statements.** Then talk with a partner. Do you agree or disagree with each statement?

1 A healthy mind   ○   ○ than a meat-based diet.

2 A vegetarian diet is healthier   ○   ○ before and after a workout.

3 Exercising 30 minutes a day   ○   ○ who is the best person to give advice.

4 It's important to stretch   ○   ○ is long enough to keep yourself fit.

5 If you're unwell, talk to a doctor, ○   ○ is just as important as a healthy body.

E **Work with a partner.** Decide if each statement is a health fact or a health myth, and circle your answer. Then check the answers on page 151. Do any surprise you?

1 Being out in cold weather causes colds.   **Fact   Myth**

2 Laughing helps increase blood flow in the body.   **Fact   Myth**

3 Chocolate causes acne, which is a common skin condition among teens.   **Fact   Myth**

4 Everyone should drink at least eight glasses of water a day.   **Fact   Myth**

5 Eating spicy food causes stomach ulcers.   **Fact   Myth**

6 Drinking water before a meal can help with weight loss.   **Fact   Myth**

Being out in cold weather causes colds, doesn't it?

I'm not so sure. I …

EDIBLE INSECTS

Macarons made with
insect powder

A ▶ 12.1 **Watch the video.** Circle **T** for true or **F** for false.

1 More than one-quarter of the world's population   **T**   **F**
currently eats insects.

2 The most popular edible insect is the beetle.   **T**   **F**

3 Most farmed insects are now used to feed people.   **T**   **F**

4 Insects are currently being used in cosmetics.   **T**   **F**

DO YOU KNOW?

Most edible ants
are said to taste like

_____.
a salt
b lemon
c pepper

B ▶ 12.1 **Watch again.** Check (✓) all the advantages of eating insects
mentioned in the video.

☐ They help improve people's memory.

☐ They are full of protein.

☐ They require less food than birds and mammals.

☐ They help people lose weight.

☐ They require less land to produce than traditional farm animals.

C Below are actual menu items containing insects (1–4). Complete these menu items with the clauses in the box (a–d). If you had to order one of these items, which would you choose?

> **a** which have been sweetened with honey
> **b** which contrast nicely with the garden greens
> **c** which is made with skim milk
> **d** which are usually filled with meat

1 **Beetle dip:** This healthy dip, _____ , gets its flavor from roasted beetles.

2 **Cricket cheesecake:** Sticky crickets, _____ , top a creamy cheesecake with a cricket flour crust.

3 **Grasshopper tacos:** Tacos, _____ , get a fresh twist when filled with fried grasshoppers.

4 **Salad with crispy worms:** Try a fresh summer salad with lightly roasted worms, _____ .

D CRITICAL THINKING Reflecting **Talk with a partner.** How do you feel about eating insects? Would you ever eat them regularly?

> **PROJECT Go online.** Find three food products for sale that contain insects. What are they, and what insects are used? Are the products advertised as containing insects?

PRONUNCIATION pausing between thought groups

A 🎧 **12.5 Listen and repeat.**

1 Large-scale insect farming / for human food / will begin soon.

2 In Uganda, / a kilogram of grasshoppers / is more expensive / than a kilogram of beef.

B 🎧 **12.6 Mark the pauses in these sentences with a slash (/).** Then listen and check your answers.

1 A healthy mind is just as important as a healthy body.

2 A vegetarian diet is healthier than a meat-based diet.

3 If you're unwell, talk to a doctor, who is the best person to give advice.

COMMUNICATION

A **Work in groups.** Imagine you have been asked to help market a new food product that contains insects. Choose one of the food products below, and note your ideas for it.

Type of food product: _____ *a breakfast cereal / an energy bar / an ice cream bar* _____

- What to name it
- Its key selling points
- What insect(s) to use
- Who to market it to

B **As a group, present your product to the class.** Then vote on which food product is most likely to become the top-selling item.

READING

A **Read the title.** In what ways is the human brain "amazing"?

B **Read the sentences below.** Check (✓) the ones you think are true. Then scan the article and check your answers.

- ☐ Your brain weighs over three kilograms.
- ☐ Eating blackberries is good for your brain.
- ☐ The structure of your brain changes every time you learn.

C **Talk with a partner.** Do you have a good memory or a bad memory? Why do you think some people have better memories than others?

A young girl undergoes a test that measures brain activity.

YOUR *AMAZING* BRAIN

A ⏵ 12.7 You carry a 1.3-kilogram mass of fatty material in your head that controls everything your body does. It lets you think, learn, create, and feel emotions. What's this amazing machine? It's your brain—a structure that scientist James Watson called "the most complex thing we have yet discovered in our universe."

Your brain is more powerful than a supercomputer.

B Imagine you see a cat about to step onto a hot stove. Your brain reads the **signals** from your eyes and quickly **calculates** when, where, and at what speed you need to run to save her. Then it tells your muscles to move. No computer can match your brain's ability to download, process, and react to the flood of information from your eyes, ears, and other sensory organs.

Neurons can send information extremely quickly.

C Your brain contains about 100 billion nerve cells called neurons. If a bee lands on your foot, sensory neurons in your skin send this information to your brain at a speed of more than 240 kilometers per hour. Your brain then uses motor neurons to send a message back to your foot: Shake the bee off quickly!

The right foods make you healthier.

D Your brain can benefit from a healthy diet, just like the rest of your body. Whole grains release glucose—the brain's main **source** of energy—into the blood slowly, helping you stay focused throughout the day. Oily fish, which contain omega-3 fatty acids, can potentially fight off brain-related illnesses such as Alzheimer's disease. Dark berries help improve brain function. Eating leafy greens **boosts** memory and learning.

Exercise helps make you smarter.

E Exercising is great for your body and can even improve your mood. But scientists have also learned that your body **produces** a chemical after you exercise that makes it easier for your brain to learn. So, the next time you can't figure out a homework problem, go out and play soccer, and then try the problem again. You might find that you're able to **solve** it!

When you learn, you change the structure of your brain.

F Riding a bike seems impossible at first, but you eventually master it. How? As you practice, your brain sends "bike riding" messages along certain neural pathways again and again, forming new connections. In fact, the structure of your brain changes every time you learn, as well as whenever you have a new thought or memory.

COMPREHENSION

IDIOM

If someone wants to "pick your brain," they'll probably _____ .
a give you a brain scan
b look at your test scores
c ask you questions

A Answer the questions about *Your Amazing Brain*.

1 **GIST** What could be another title for the article?

   a Understanding the Brain and How It Works

   b New Trends in Brain Research

   c How to Train Your Brain to Think Faster

2 **VOCABULARY** In paragraph B, *the flood of information* means _____ of information.

   a a lack   b a variety   c a huge amount

3 **DETAIL** According to the article, which of the following is NOT true?

   a The brain's processing power allows you to react quickly in an emergency situation.

   b The human brain contains about 100 billion neurons.

   c The brain gets most of its energy from omega-3 fatty acids.

4 **INFERENCE** If you were stuck on a homework problem, the author might suggest _____ .

   a going to the gym

   b playing a musical instrument

   c doing a crossword puzzle

5 **COHESION** The following sentence would best be placed at the end of which paragraph?

   A recent report suggests that a daily serving of spinach could make your brain 11 years younger.

   a paragraph A   b paragraph D   c paragraph F

B Complete the summary below. Use the words in the box. One word is extra.

| connections | food | glucose | illnesses | neurons | think |

Your brain is incredibly powerful. It allows you to [1] _____, to feel, and to learn. When you sense an emergency, your brain reads the signals and uses your motor [2] _____ to tell your muscles to move. But the brain needs the right [3] _____ to function well. Whole grains, oily fish, berries, and leafy greens all help improve brain function and possibly fight off certain [4] _____. Exercising also helps make it easier for you to learn. Every time you learn something new, the structure of your brain changes as it forms new [5] _____.

C CRITICAL THINKING Comparing and Contrasting Talk with a partner. Do you think male and female brains are better at different tasks? If so, what kinds of tasks?

VOCABULARY

A **Find the words below in the article.** Then complete the information using the words in the box.

> boost   calculate   produce   signals   solve   source

The human brain is a ^{1} _____ of wonder. Check out these facts about the brain:

- The brain interprets pain ^{2} _____ , but it doesn't actually feel pain.

- The brain can combine individual memories to ^{3} _____ problems.

- Playing classical music to babies can potentially ^{4} _____ their brain power.

- Even while asleep, your brain can ^{5} _____ enough energy to power a 25-watt light bulb.

- It's possible to ^{6} _____ numbers in your head faster by learning a few mental tricks.

B **Read the information below.** Then circle the correct answers.

> The word root *sens-* means "feel." Many words can be formed using this root, such as:
>
> | | | | |
> |---|---|---|---|
> | *sense* | *sensor* | *sensible* | *sensation* |
> | *senses* | *sensory* | *sensitive* | *sensational* |

1 Which of your five **senses** / **sensors** do you think is the strongest?

2 It would have been more **sense** / **sensible** to save the money than to spend it all on shoes.

3 After his eye surgery, he was very **sensitive** / **sensational** to light for a few days.

4 The accident caused a loss of **sensory** / **sensation** in her right foot.

WRITING

A **Read the paragraph.**

B **Choose a health-related goal.** How do you plan to achieve this goal? Note some ideas.

C **Write an action plan.** Create a step-by-step plan for achieving your goal. Use your notes from **B** to help you.

timezones.com/forum

My goal is to go to sleep early every night so that I can have more energy to study and play sports during the day. To do this, I will set a regular bedtime. I also plan to stop …

FOOD **ALLERGIES**

Before You Watch

The bold words and phrases below are used in the video. Complete the definitions. Circle the correct answers.

1 If someone is **allergic to** a food, they *can / cannot* eat it safely.

2 People with good personal **hygiene** keep themselves very *clean / well-fed*.

3 If you are **exposed to** a disease, you *could / definitely won't* get it.

4 Your **immune system** helps you *digest food / fight off disease*.

While You Watch

A ▶ 12.2 **Watch Part 1 of the video.** Check (✓) the things that are true about Xaviar.

☐ He's allergic to tree nuts.

☐ He's not allergic to eggs anymore.

☐ He's educated at home instead of at school.

☐ He can have an allergic reaction through skin contact.

B ▶ 12.3 **Watch Part 2 of the video.** Circle the correct answers.

1 The hygiene theory suggests that living in an environment that is **too clean / not clean enough** can cause children to develop allergies.

2 Dr. Robert Wood is especially concerned about the **possibility of an accidental allergic reaction / high cost of new treatments**.

3 Near the end of the video, Xaviar demonstrates how to **put on an oxygen mask / give himself an injection**.

After You Watch

Discuss with a partner. Below are a few ways to protect children with food allergies. What might be some advantages or disadvantages of each approach?

• Ban the top allergy-causing foods (e.g., milk, wheat, nuts) from school cafeterias.

• Encourage children with food allergies to sit separately from other kids.

• Require children with food allergies to wear ID bracelets stating their allergies.

• Require menus in restaurants to list all the ingredients in dishes.

A Look at the word groups. Cross out the odd item in each group.

1 **vegetables:** carrots spinach ~~shellfish~~

2 **fruits:** onions papayas mangoes

3 **grains:** wheat milk oatmeal

4 **red meats:** chicken lamb beef

5 **processed foods:** frozen pizzas apples potato chips

B Complete the sentences. Circle the correct answers.

1 These crickets are **too / enough** salty for me.

2 Your sister buys organic food, **does / doesn't** she?

3 My mother doesn't enjoy **to cook / cooking** very much.

4 These strawberries are not as **fresh / fresher** as those.

5 My friend, **who / which** is an aerobics instructor, is in great shape.

Common food allergens

C Complete the sentences. Use the words in the box. One word is extra.

> sensation   sensational   sense   senses   sensible

1 It's not easy to lose weight. Try to be _____ about your food choices.

2 When I entered the room, I didn't _____ anything was wrong.

3 She felt a burning _____ in her throat.

4 Of my five _____, I think I appreciate taste the most!

SELF CHECK   Now I can ...

☐ talk about health and nutrition

☐ use previously learned language

☐ discuss what makes the human brain special

UNIT 3 LANGUAGE FOCUS

Work with a partner. Copy the words you wrote on page 33 in the blanks below. Then take turns reading each problem and evaluating the advice.

Problem 1:

I want to dress better. My [1] _____ always gives me advice. He always says, "If I were you, I'd wear more colorful [2] _____ and [3] _____. You'll look nicer." He also says that [4] _____ is a good color for me. Should I take his advice? Do you have better advice for me?

Problem 2:

I want to have a healthier lifestyle. My [5] _____ says I should eat more [6] _____ and less [7] _____. She also says I could do more sports, like [8] _____. Is this good advice? What do you suggest I do to have a healthier lifestyle?

UNIT 7 LANGUAGE FOCUS

Student A: Read your mystery story to Student B. Discuss what you think happened.

Who made the stone balls, and why?

In the 1930s, farm workers in Costa Rica discovered a collection of over 300 stone balls. The stone balls date from the 7th to the 16th centuries, and are almost perfectly round. Some are the size of a tennis ball, while others are much larger—up to two meters wide. They were made by humans, but no one knows why. What was their purpose?

UNIT 11 COMMUNICATION

Team A: Read the information below.

You **support** the ban. Think of ways the ban will benefit teachers and students. Come up with a list of arguments. Think about how cell phones can negatively affect students in the classroom. Also, think of points to counter Team B's possible arguments.

Follow these steps:

1 Team A: Present your arguments.
2 Team B: Counter Team A's arguments, and present your arguments.
3 Team A: Counter Team B's arguments, and summarize your arguments.
4 Team B: Summarize your arguments.
5 Discuss which team you think won the debate.

UNIT 4 LANGUAGE FOCUS

Student A: Skim the news article. Ask your partner questions to complete the article. Use the words in parentheses to help you form questions.

A Cry for Help

A baby manatee calls out for her mother. She doesn't hear any reply. A man finds the baby and calls a rescue service for help. He knows the baby won't survive on its own.

A rescue team rushes to the river. They lower a [1] _____ (**what**) into the water. They manage to catch the baby manatee. They then carry her to their vehicle. Here, she is placed in a pool and then driven to a local zoo. When they arrive, the vet gives the baby manatee a checkup. The examination shows that the creature, now named Kee, is underweight. To increase her weight, Kee is given milk [3] _____ (**how often**).

The following month, an adult manatee arrives at the zoo. This animal, named Della, has injuries caused by an accident with a boat. A few days later, Della gives birth to a baby named Pal. This gives Virginia Edmonds, a caretaker at the zoo, an idea. She hopes Della will care for Kee like her baby. So the three manatees are placed [5] _____ (**where**). Shortly after, Della begins to feed Kee. To everyone's joy, Della accepts Kee as her own. They're all one family now.

After four months, Della has recovered. It's time for her and her family to return to the wild. They are released into the river. "Kee is back where she belongs," says Edmonds.

UNIT 12 LANGUAGE FOCUS

Answers:

1 Myth—Viruses cause colds and the flu, not the weather. However, some viruses are more likely to spread at cooler temperatures. Cold weather may also weaken your ability to fight off illness.
2 Fact
3 Myth—There is no evidence that cocoa beans, from which chocolate is made, cause acne. However, a high-sugar or high-fat diet can increase your chances of developing the skin condition.
4 Myth—Everyone's water needs vary depending on their age, weight, level of physical activity, and the climate they live in. Also, fruits such as watermelons and strawberries, for example, contain a lot of water. These food sources contribute to your daily water intake.
5 Myth—Most stomach ulcers are caused by a particular bacterial infection or by long-term use of certain drugs. Spicy food does not cause ulcers. However, it can make existing ulcers worse.
6 Fact

UNIT 4 LANGUAGE FOCUS

Student B: Skim the news article. Ask your partner questions to complete the article. Use the words in parentheses to help you form questions.

A Cry for Help

A baby manatee calls out for her mother. She doesn't hear any reply. A man finds the baby and calls a rescue service for help. He knows the baby won't survive on its own.

A rescue team rushes to the river. They lower a small net into the water. They manage to catch the baby manatee. They then carry her to their vehicle. Here, she is placed in a pool and then driven to [2] _____ (**where**). When they arrive, the vet gives the baby manatee a checkup. The examination shows that the creature, now named Kee, is underweight. To increase her weight, Kee is given milk every three hours.

The following month, [4] _____ (**what**) arrives at the zoo. This animal, named Della, has injuries caused by an accident with a boat. A few days later, Della gives birth to a baby named Pal. This gives Virginia Edmonds, a caretaker at the zoo, an idea. She hopes Della will care for Kee like her baby. So the three manatees are placed in the same pool. Shortly after, Della begins to feed Kee. To everyone's joy, Della accepts Kee as her own. They're all one family now.

After four months, Della has recovered. It's time for her and her family to return to the wild. They are released [6] _____ (**where**). "Kee is back where she belongs," says Edmonds.

UNIT 11 COMMUNICATION

Team B: Read the information below.

You **don't support** the ban. Think of ways the ban wouldn't be good for teachers and students. Come up with a list of arguments. Think about how cell phones can contribute to learning. Also, think of points to counter Team A's possible arguments.

Follow these steps:

1 Team A: Present your arguments.
2 Team B: Counter Team A's arguments, and present your arguments.
3 Team A: Counter Team B's arguments, and summarize your arguments.
4 Team B: Summarize your arguments.
5 Discuss which team you think won the debate.

UNIT 5 LANGUAGE FOCUS

Student A: Ask your partner questions about balloons to complete the information below.
Answer your partner's questions about dice.

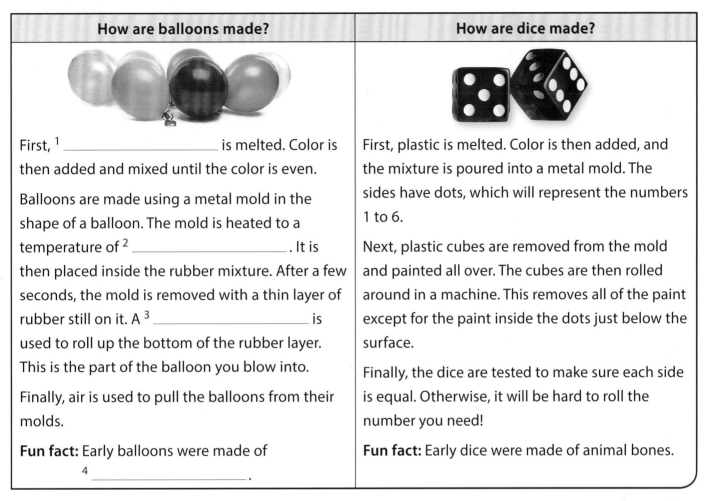

How are balloons made?	How are dice made?
First, [1] _____ is melted. Color is then added and mixed until the color is even.	First, plastic is melted. Color is then added, and the mixture is poured into a metal mold. The sides have dots, which will represent the numbers 1 to 6.
Balloons are made using a metal mold in the shape of a balloon. The mold is heated to a temperature of [2] _____ . It is then placed inside the rubber mixture. After a few seconds, the mold is removed with a thin layer of rubber still on it. A [3] _____ is used to roll up the bottom of the rubber layer. This is the part of the balloon you blow into.	Next, plastic cubes are removed from the mold and painted all over. The cubes are then rolled around in a machine. This removes all of the paint except for the paint inside the dots just below the surface.
Finally, air is used to pull the balloons from their molds.	Finally, the dice are tested to make sure each side is equal. Otherwise, it will be hard to roll the number you need!
Fun fact: Early balloons were made of [4] _____ .	**Fun fact:** Early dice were made of animal bones.

UNIT 7 LANGUAGE FOCUS

Student B: Read your mystery story to Student A. Discuss what you think happened.

Why are dogs jumping to their deaths?

In Dumbarton, Scotland, there's an old, high bridge from which many dogs have jumped. Since the 1950s, around 600 dogs have jumped off this bridge. About 50 have died. They all jump from the same place, without warning, usually on a clear day. Most are dog breeds that have long noses. Why do the dogs jump?

UNIT 5 LANGUAGE FOCUS

Student B: Ask your partner questions about dice to complete the information below.
Answer your partner's questions about balloons.

How are balloons made?	How are dice made?
First, rubber is melted. Color is then added and mixed until the color is even. Balloons are made using a metal mold in the shape of a balloon. The mold is heated to a temperature of about 90°C. It is then placed inside the rubber mixture. After a few seconds, the mold is removed with a thin layer of rubber still on it. A brush is used to roll up the bottom of the rubber layer. This is the part of the balloon you blow into. Finally, air is used to pull the balloons from their molds. **Fun fact:** Early balloons were made of animal intestines.	First, [5] _____ is melted. Color is then added, and the mixture is poured into a [6] _____ . The sides have dots, which will represent the numbers 1 to 6. Next, plastic cubes are removed from the mold and painted all over. The cubes are then rolled around in a [7] _____ . This removes all of the paint except for the paint inside the dots just below the surface. Finally, the dice are tested to make sure each side is equal. Otherwise, it will be hard to roll the number you need! **Fun fact:** Early dice were made of [8] _____ .

UNIT 6 COMMUNICATION

Group A: Choose an animal below. Combine two facts using a relative clause. Don't say the name of the animal. After Group B has made a guess, move on to another animal. Take turns giving clues and guessing. The group with the higher number of correct guesses at the end wins.

Albatross (bird)

Lifespan in the wild:
About 50 years

Habitat:
Southern Ocean and North Pacific Ocean

Interesting fact 1: It drinks saltwater.

Interesting fact 2: It sometimes floats on the sea's surface.

Emperor penguin (bird)

Lifespan in the wild:
15 to 20 years

Habitat:
Antarctica

Interesting fact 1: It can dive 565 meters and stay underwater for more than 20 minutes.

Interesting fact 2: It only has one chick a year.

Bottlenose dolphin (mammal)

Lifespan in the wild:
45 to 50 years

Habitat:
Warm and tropical waters around the world

Interesting fact 1: It can swim 30 kilometers an hour and jump almost 5 meters out of the water.

Interesting fact 2: It only lets one-half of its brain sleep at a time.

Northern fur seal (mammal)

Lifespan in the wild:
Up to 26 years

Habitat:
Cold waters of the North Pacific Ocean

Interesting fact 1: It has large eyes that let it see well underwater and at night.

Interesting fact 2: It has huge flippers that help it stay cool.

Dugong (mammal)

Lifespan in the wild:
About 70 years

Habitat:
Warm coastal waters of the Red Sea, Indian Ocean, and Pacific Ocean

Interesting fact 1: It is related to elephants.

Interesting fact 2: It was sometimes mistaken for a mermaid by sailors.

Hermit crab (shellfish)

Lifespan in the wild:
Up to 30 years

Habitat:
Saltwater from shallow coastal areas to deep seas worldwide

Interesting fact 1: It is active at night.

Interesting fact 2: It often climbs over another of its kind instead of going around.

Group B's animals:

leatherback turtle	sea otter	manta ray
saltwater crocodile	stonefish	whale shark

UNIT 6 COMMUNICATION

Group B: Choose an animal below. Combine two facts using a relative clause. Don't say the name of the animal. After Group A has made a guess, move on to another animal. Take turns giving clues and guessing. The group with the higher number of correct guesses at the end wins.

Leatherback turtle (reptile)

Lifespan in the wild:
About 45 years

Habitat:
Tropical and warm waters of the Atlantic, Pacific, and Indian Oceans, but seen in colder oceans, too

Interesting fact 1: It buries its eggs in the sand.

Interesting fact 2: It is endangered.

Sea otter (mammal)

Lifespan in the wild:
Up to 23 years

Habitat:
Coasts of the Pacific Ocean in North America and Asia

Interesting fact 1: It has to eat three hours a day to stay warm.

Interesting fact 2: It uses rocks to break open shellfish.

Manta ray (fish)

Lifespan in the wild:
Up to 20 years

Habitat:
Warm waters, often near coral reefs

Interesting fact 1: It looks like a blanket.

Interesting fact 2: It eats about 13 percent of its body weight in food each week.

Stonefish (fish)

Lifespan in the wild:
Not known

Habitat:
On coral reefs and near rocks, in warm and tropical waters of the Indian and Pacific Oceans

Interesting fact 1: It is one of the most poisonous fish in the world.

Interesting fact 2: It can live outside of the ocean for 20 hours.

Saltwater crocodile (reptile)

Lifespan in the wild:
Up to 70 years

Habitat:
Freshwater and saltwater areas of eastern India, Southeast Asia, and northern Australia

Interesting fact 1: It kills one to two people every year in Australia.

Interesting fact 2: It sometimes swims far out to sea.

Whale shark (fish)

Lifespan in the wild:
60 to 100 years

Habitat:
Warm and tropical waters all over the world

Interesting fact 1: It looks dangerous but is actually very gentle.

Interesting fact 2: It can only reproduce when it is about 30 years old.

Group A's animals:

albatross	emperor penguin	bottlenose dolphin
dugong	northern fur seal	hermit crab

WORD LIST

Word	Unit	Word	Unit	Word	Unit
abandon	7	connect	11	goods	8
ability	3	council	1	gradually	3
about	6	counsel	1	grant a wish	10
advice	1	crime	11	hang	4
advise	1	curious	9	help	4
affect	1	cut	11	hold the record	2
afraid	9	damage	6	horrible	9
announce	2	dangerous	4	horror	9
appeal	9	defeat	2	hurricane	7
appear	1	determination	2	hurt	11
around	6	distance	2	identify	9
arrive	4	dying wish	10	imagine	7
attract	6	effect	1	in record time	2
avalanche	7	enter	4	individual	5
average	1	event	10	inspire	10
blame	11	eventually	1	invention	10
blizzard	7	experiment	11	investigate	4
board	8	export	8	journey	8
boost	12	factor	9	lack of	7
break the record	2	fascination	9	leader	1
bring	4	financial record	2	luggage	8
calculate	12	first-class	8	make a wish	10
car	8	flood	7	make of	3
challenge	3	frightened	4	make out	3
cheer	4	global	5	make up	3
collapse	7	global awareness	5	make up for	3
combine	5	global brand	5	medical record	2
come	4	global network	5	mood	9
complex	5	global warming	5	more than	6

CREDITS

Photo Credits

Art Credits

ACKNOWLEDGMENTS

Thank you to the educators who provided invaluable feedback during the development of *Time Zones:*

ADVISORS

Apryl Peredo, Teacher, Hongo Junior and Senior High School, Tokyo
Carolina Espinosa, Coordinator, Associação Cultural Brasil-Estados Unidos, Brazil
Chary Aguirre, Academic and English Coordinator, Colegio Muñoz, Mexico
Elizabeth Yonetsugi, Global Program Manager, Berlitz Japan, Tokyo
Helena Mesquita Bizzarri, Academic Coordinator, SESI, Brazil
Hiroyo Noguchi, Lecturer, Momoyama Gakuin University (St. Andrew's University), Osaka
Isabella Alvim, Academic Coordinator, Instituto Brasil-Estados Unidos (IBEU) - Rio de Janeiro, Brazil
Kota Ikeshima, Teacher, Shibuya Junior & Senior High School, Tokyo
Nelly Romero, Head of Academic Design and Projects, Instituto Cultural Peruano Norteamericano (ICPNA), Peru
Nhi Nguyen, Program Manager, Vietnam USA Society English Centers (VUS), Ho Chi Minh City
Sabrina Hong, Education and Training Manager, Aston English, Xi'an
Sean Patterson, Global Programs Manager, Kanto Gakuin Mutsuura Junior and Senior High School, Yokohama
Sílvia de Melo Caldas, Course Designer, Casa Thomas Jefferson, Brazil
Sophy Oum, Academic Coordinator, ACE Cambodia, Phnom Penh
Wenjing Luo, Research and Development Manager, CERNET Education, Beijing
Yu-Chih (Portia) Chang, Head Teacher, Start Education Experts, Taipei

REVIEWERS

LATIN AMERICA

Adriene Zigaib, Brazil
Ana Paula Marques Migliari, School Connect, Brazil
Anna Lúcia Seabra Mendes, Casa Thomas Jefferson, Brazil
Auricea Bacelar, Top Seven Idiomas, Brazil
Barbara Souza, EM Maria Quiteria, Brazil
Daniela Coelho, SayOk! English School, Brazil
Gilberto Dalla Verde Junior, Colégio Tomas Agostinho, Brazil
Isabella Campos, Instituto Brasil-Estados Unidos (IBEU) - Rio de Janeiro, Brazil
Jessica Yanett Carrillo Torres, John Nash School, Peru
Juliana Pinho, Instituto Brasil-Estados Unidos (IBEU), Brazil
Juliana Ribeiro Lima Passos, CIEP 117 Carlos Drummond de Andrade Brasil-USA, Brazil
Katherin Ortiz Torres, Santa Angela Merici School, Peru
Kathleen Isabelle Tavares da Silva, Inglês Para Todos, Brazil
Larissa Pizzano Platinetti Vieira, Centro Cultural Brasil - Estados Unidos (CCBEU) Guarapuava, Brazil
Laura Raffo Pires, Extra English, Brazil
Luis Sergio Moreira da Silva, Webster, Brazil
María del Rosario Aguirre Román, Colegio Muñoz, Mexico
Maria Helena Querioz e Lima, Cultura Inglesa Uberlândia, Brazil
Mónica Rosales, Instituto Franklin de Veracruz, Mexico
Natasha Freitas Silva, ATW English, Brazil
Natasha Pereira, ATW English, Brazil
Neri Zabdi Barrenechea Garcia, Welcome English, Peru
Patricia Perez, Colégio Martin Miguel de Guemes, Argentina
Raphael Fonseca Porto, Casa Thomas Jefferson, Brazil
Renata Lucia Cardoso, Instituto Natural de Desenvolvimento Infantil, Brazil
Roosevelt Oliveira, Coopling, Brazil
Samuel Nicacio Silva Santos, Casa Thomas Jefferson, Brazil
Silvia Castilho Cintra, Ingles com Silvia, Brazil
Silvia Martínez Marín, I.E.P. Henri La Fontaine, Peru
Stela Foley, Brazil

EUROPE AND AFRICA

Theresa Taylor, American Language Center, Morocco

ASIA

Andrew Duenas, ILA Vietnam, Ho Chi Minh City
Camille Nota, Berlitz Japan, Tokyo
Dan Quinn, Jakarta Japanese School, Jakarta
Edwin G Wiehe, Shitennoji Junior and Senior High School, Osaka
Georges Erhard, ILA Vietnam, Ho Chi Minh City
Haruko Morimoto, Kanda Gaigo Career College, Tokyo
Mai Thị Ngọc Anh, ILA Vietnam, Ho Chi Minh City
Masaki Aso, Japan University of Economics, Fukuoka
Paul Adams, Ming Dao High School, Taichung
Samuel Smith, Jakarta Japanese School, Jakarta
Sayidah Salim, Dian Didatika Junior High School, Jakarta
Shogo Minagawa, Doshisha Junior High School, Kyoto
Trevor Goodwin, IBL English, Wonju
Yoko Sakurai, Nagoya Gakuin University, Nagoya